014434272 Liverpool Univ

KU-288-379

University of Liverpool

Withdrawn from stack

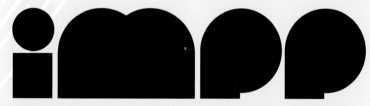

International Manual of Planning Practice

Judith Ryser and Teresa Franchini Editors

CONTENT

Acknowledgements

We wish to express our gratitude to the many persons and institutions which supported the production of this new edition of the International Manual of Planning Practice over four years.

First we are thanking ISOCARP for inviting us to edit this new book and CD, following the great undertaking of Adriana dal Cin and Derek Lyddon who initiated the idea together with Javier de Mesones and produced previous editions. Our gratitude goes to them for leaving an invaluable heritage.

Most importantly, we convey our thanks to the authors of this Manual from all over the world who put enormous efforts into assisting the planning profession and the development world generally by contributing the most valuable asset of the IMPP, their knowledge and experience.

We also thank the institutions and their collaborators who gave their time and ingenuity in finding ways to bring this Manual into being: the ISOCARP General Secretary, Pablo Vaggione for trying to find a publisher; the ISOCARP Vice President Manfred Schrenk for his technological advice; the ISOCARP Secretariat and the Sitges Project Office for distributing the publication; the Polytechnic School of the CEU San Pablo University for academic assistance; the Commonwealth Association of Planners for establishing professional contacts, Temanova Consulting for sponsoring the translation of some entries and in particular the Fundacion Metropoli for inspiration and support. The ISOCARP United Kingdom Delegation deserves a special mention for its constant encouragement and above all the Scottish Executive Development Department, the Royal Town Planning Institute and Michael Collins for their financial assistance without which this publication would not have been possible.

We want to thank other people who so generously contributed their time to the editing process without any personal gain: Michael Collins, Peter Robinson, Kate Ralfe, Clive Richardson and Ines Sosa, to mention but the inner circle.

Finally, colleagues and friends gave us precious moral support, an essential ingredient in this kind of task: Manuel Ballester, Chris Gossop, James McKinnon, Vincent Goodstadt, Judith Eversley, Leonora Shapland, Iniaki Lopez de Maturana, Estefania Chavez and many others.

The editors, *Judith Ryser & Teresa Franchini, Madrid, September 2008.*

Foreword

I am pleased to greet the new edition of the International Manual of Planning Practice - IMPP - and to first of all congratulate the editors for this important publication. Their efforts spanning over more than five years have now come to a successful result. I would also like to take this opportunity to thank the authors from all continents for their contributions to a compendium with some over one hundred entries, which reflects the complexity of the planning systems and practices worldwide. I would also like to thank the generous sponsors and planning colleagues from the UK, Spain and South Africa who have assisted this publication both financially and in kind and made it possible.

ISOCARP took an early initiative in 1992 to illustrate the planning processes in its International Manual of Planning Practice updated in 1995, 1998 and 2001. I would acknowledge the great effort of the previous editors, and my predecessors as ISOCARP presidents, Adriana dal Cin and Derek Lyddon. Their work has been the basis for this new, expanded edition of IMPP that gives a fresh insight into administrative structures, planning systems and physical development processes of cities and regions in the 21st century.

The innovative aspect of this unique new source of information is its worldwide scope and its emphasis on the relationship between the planning system and its application in practice. Another welcome new contribution is the essay of the editors which discusses planning processes at the dawn of the 21st century highlighting similarities, differences and best practices against the background of the spatial development of cities, regions and nation states.

May I wish this new edition to have the success it deserves.

Pierre Laconte
President of ISOCARP

The long view of IMPP

Based on the simplistic premise that "planning is making arrangements for the future", it became clear from the early days of congresses and papers of the International Society of City and Regional Planners (ISOCARP) that for each country the question arose: "what type of arrangement and for the future of what?"

It was in conversation with Adriana dal Cin at the 1988 Congress that she suggested that it should be possible for each country to record the answers to these questions and then to compare their approaches. This she did in Volume One of the Manual, published in 1989, and in Volume Four, in 2001, she provided a remarkable glossary and comparisons, covering 26 countries.

Mobilising members of ISOCARP and professional friends, experienced and young planners alike, she persevered over three years initially to turn this project into reality. UNESCO with which ISOCARP enjoys accreditation status was very supportive and valued in particular the dissemination of this knowledge to less developed countries. It fitted the objectives of MOST, UNESCO's Management of Social Transformations programme which was training young city professionals to cope with the urban societies of the 21st century, to humanise cities and to promote and create a sustainable human habitat. Democratic management of the built environment and its development by means of innovating the planning process and fostering creative negotiation mechanisms for the various urban actors remains at the heart of this fifth edition of the Manual which contributes knowledge and critical reflection toward humanising urban living conditions.

In the light of exponential urban growth the management of scarce resources and the natural environment have moved centre stage also in the spatial planning world, especially now that the majority of humanity resides in cities. Thus, my Scottish fellow professionals and the Royal Town Planning Institute found it worth their while to support the IMPP at present.

The new IMPP offers the diversity of over one hundred countries, thanks to the outstanding efforts of Judith Ryser and Teresa Franchini, whose new Template for the Manual is a major contribution to the life, work and future Manuals of Isocarp.

Derek Lyddon
Originator and joint editor of four editions of IMPP
Past President of ISOCARP

This book is about the planning system and its application in practice. It constitutes a compendium on planning of interest to practising planners in both the public and the private sector, as well as to other built environment professionals. It is also a reference book for academics and students and provides basic information for planners, developers and investors who intend to operate abroad.

IMPP gives readers a comparative overview of planning worldwide provided by experienced planning practitioners and academics in five continents. One hundred case studies in Africa, America, Asia, Australasia and Europe give a comprehensive panorama of the regulated development process and puts it into the perspective of real world experiences, structured into:

- *General country information*: description of the general country information (text, diagrams and maps dealing with location, size, characteristics of the country, population, GDP, etc.)
- *Planning framework:* an overview of the administrative structure, the administrative competences for planning, the legal framework of spatial, physical, strategic, structural, social, economic, environmental planning, the planning and implementation instruments and the development control mechanisms
- *Planning process*: comments on the planning system, plan making, development enforcement, participation and appeal and initiatives outside planning procedures
- *Evaluation*: critical analysis of the application of the planning system in practice, focusing on the gap between planning legislation and physical development and the future prospects of the planning system, apart from other relevant comments.

The information provided by the authors forms the basis of the concise synthesis of each country produced by the editors, together with an essay on the state of the art and future outlook of planning. The full papers with illustrations produced by the authors, an international list of planning contacts, and other relevant material is included in the CD as part of this publication in interactive mode.

About the sources of the data used in this book
- General country information: Total area, total population, population growth, unemployment rate, GDP, GDP per capita and GDP growth rate. The CIA World Factbook https://www.cia.gov/library/publications/the-world-factbook
- Settlements structure: Capital city and second city, including population. Infoplease: http://www.infoplease.com. Extra info: City population: Thomas Brinkhoff: City Population, http://www.citypopulation.de
- Population density : Own data
- Urban population : Tiscali reference: http://www.tiscali.co.uk.

The World of Planning and its Future

Purpose of the Essay

Judith Ryser and Teresa Franchini, editors

The purpose of this evidence based essay is to identify current trends of planning and single out similarities as a contribution to practising planners - as well as professionals of the built environment generally - to reflect on the relation between regulated and spontaneous development processes. Experiences written by practising planners from all five continents may be useful for planning professionals when dealing with geo-political, socio-economic, environmental and physical transformations which affect both planning practice and the planning profession.

The International Manuel of Planning Practice (IMPP) focuses on spatial development in its broadest sense and the role of planning in steering and assisting it. It should shed light on the evolution and future prospects of planning in today's turbulent world. Evidence from one hundred and one countries worldwide, presented in this new edition is used as the source for this essay, together with the editors' own research. It reveals how widespread some well known but seldom resolved planning problems are, but it also contains many surprises and especially innovative initiatives, often hatched under most challenging conditions.

Planning has not been standing still since the last editions of IMPP, and planners themselves have continued to be instrumental in exploring new approaches to a more effective development process, as demonstrated in "Four Decades of Knowledge Creation and Sharing"[1] . Focusing on the second half of the 20th century while also referring back to previous history the IMPP contributions show that physical development tends to follow its own momentum, depending on the geo-political context, development pressures, economic conditions, political powers and the effectiveness of planning. The essay discusses the interaction of these complex forces in creating a tripartite contradiction between formal planning systems, their application in practice and development processes occurring outside these controls. It concludes with implications for planners and their knowledge base.

Context of the development process
Settlement structure and development, with and despite planning

1.1 What is Planning and Since When?
A glance at history with focus on cities

There are conflicting schools of thought about the origins of planning. Over millennia, societies invented tools to dominated nature, the ultimate goal of the enlightenment philosophy.[2] For some, even cave men had to plan to overcome nature. A glance at Benevolo's 'History of the City'[3] shows that from the New Stone Age onwards - about 10'000 years ago - when mankind started to cultivate land, became sedentary and produced surplus collectively it created permanent settlements.

Cities arose when societies were planning their own development. In the Near East, considered the origin of urban culture, surplus was distributed and traded in planned cities under an emerging ruling class which ensured technical and military hegemony over the countryside.[4] Walled capitals of empires such as Babylon were built around 2000 BC as seats of priests and kings, contrary to Egypt's physical separation between the living and the dead. Cities were not confined to Europe and emerged in all parts of the world. The Harappa in the Indus Valley had built dense cities with physical infrastructures three millennia ago and thirty centuries ago cities were instrumental in supporting Chinese codified law, while in Meso-America places of worship preceded the colonial cities.

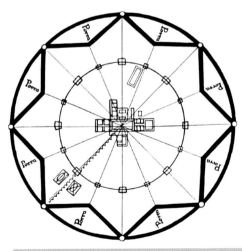
One of many images of the ideal city, Filarete

Many consider the free 'democratic city' in Ancient Greece as the origin of planned civilised coexistence. Its planning criteria were a single entity with a public realm within its confines, leaving nature untouched outside, and maintaining contained growth at a human scale. From a humanistic standpoint Richard Sennett[5] emphasises the symbolic and real links of cities with the people who inhabit them, including those without rights to the city. The Roman, Medieval and Renaissance cities developed organically from there, until the industrial revolution and its ensuing massive population increase ran rough-shots through their ordered concepts. Ildefons Cerda and Arturo Soria in Spain both planned large scale city expansions, the former the Barcelona grid and the latter a linear city outside Madrid, while Reinhard Baumeister in Germany brought together technical, regulatory and economic consideration in city development and formalised the planning profession. Peter Hall's "Cities in Civilisation"[6] provides a comprehensive insight into the evolution of cities in Europe up to what he believes is their golden age to come.

Idelfonso Cerda, Barcelona grid

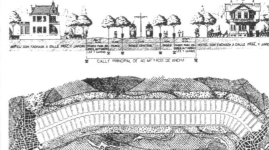

Arturo Soria linear city Madrid

In response to the rise of capitalism and urbanisation in the western world, physical planning attempted to bring order to liberal development.[7] Health and hygiene criteria generated 19th century planning during industrialisation, while municipal socialism and post first world war planning[8] provided much of today's hard and soft urban infrastructure. However, alternative models— both philanthropic utopian movements led by Owen, Fourier, Garnier and many others, and speculative development — Ebenezer Howard's garden cities realised being a prime example — were intertwined and developed alongside the formally planned world. In their own ways, all three approaches responded to unsuitable settlements spawned by rapid urban growth, as well as to new urban demands emerging from changing attitudes about the quality of life and its physical setting.

Ebenezer Howard garden city concept

Physical planning came into its own more generally after the second world war when a devastated world was in need of reconstruction. Inspired by architects, the Modern Movement, the CIAMs[9] and the Athens Charter[10] influenced urban design and planning worldwide. Planners revived such a federating instrument in 1998, when the European Council of Town Planners (ECTP) drafted a new Charter, a planners' vision for sustainable cities and regions of the 21st century.[11]

These mainly Eurocentric ways of planning were diffused through the process of colonisation but gave rise to very different developments over time and after the colonial era. A perspective from the developing world, the Caribbean and South America, illustrates these diverging trends.

1.2 The Latin American perspective

This point of view constitutes a counterpart to the conventional presentation of how planning has evolved and spread through the world. There are clearly two phases which marked the evolution of the spatial development process in the developing world. Latin American which has been colonised early differs from Asia or Africa. Its two distinct phases from the colonial times to the independence era and its development, economic models and cities in the 20th century provide a specific reality of the developing world with which globalisation is confronted at present also in planning matters.

1.2.1   A planning legislation for a new world

Cities were a key element in the process of colonisation after the conquest of the American continent in 1492, divided two years later into the Portuguese and the Spanish area. While in future Brazil there were no rules for the design of the new cities, in the Spanish speaking world Ferdinand the Catholic issued several instructions early in 1513 to regulate the cities from the beginning, using the grid as a basic pattern and the square as the focal point. His interest in planned cities was followed by his son, Philip II, who in 1573 enacted a Real Decree to lay down planning conditions. Known as "The Indians Laws", this decree defines a code of urbanism aimed to control urban practice in the new territories and regulating the shapes and sizes of any parts of the city - plazas, streets, plots, public facilities and communal spaces.[12]

Very little remains from Pre-Colombian urbanism. The magnificent ceremonial centres of the Mayas, Incas and Aztecs were replaced by hundreds of regular small settlements founded on the edge of the continent to favour the transfer of raw materials and products to the metropolises overseas. The enormous distances among the cities, the scarcity

La Plata Bolivia 1750

of communications and the loose control exerted by a complex administrative structure dependent on Madrid and Lisbon, made the cities autonomous entities where the political and economic powers resided. This situation persisted after the independence process which split the region into the present countries between 1810 and 1831.

1.2.2   The new republics and the process of urbanisation

Independence brought very few changes to the inherited spatial urban pattern composed by a rim of urban centres of different ranges on the continental borders and huge inhabited inland regions. The original vocation of the continent as exporter of agricultural products for the industrialised world remained, how linked to other external developed economies.[13]

The most impressive feature of this period in territorial terms was the reinforcement of the capital cities, favoured by their location, political influence and growing concentration of activities and population. On the other hand, the need to include the vacant inner areas to the economic dynamic favoured the foundation of new settlements and the construction of transport means – roads and railroads - to move the agro production to the main cities. The new territorial structure defined a network of minor and intermediate nuclei linked to the distribution centres surrounded by ample rural areas. The lack of influential intermediate cities and connections among the regions gave rise to the uneven distribution of population and wealth. The hypertrophy of the capital city due to its economic and political supremacy, strengthening the centrality inherited from the colonial times, and the dichotomy between the "city" and the "country", were the main outcomes of this model of spatial organisation.

1.2.3   Local government and the city

The organisation of the modern states stressed the importance of cities, in general ruled by representatives nominated by the central government, a fact which contradicts the workings of democratic traditions. The scarce political representation of the local level within the global state organisation, linked to precarious technical and financial conditions, prevented the development of a local administration, independently of the national government mandates. The capacity to undertake public works was reduced to few initiatives and gave rise to the main characteristic of the Latin American cities: a historic core surrounded by widespread informal settlements.

1.2.4   Contemporary planning system in practice[14]

There are two planning roots in the region: the ex-British colonies which follow the British planning system and countries which have organised their own planning systems based on different planning experiences influenced by France, England, the USA and Spain. There are two different situations: countries with general planning frameworks and those controlling physical development through sectoral legislation. Chile was first to approve a National Planning Act in 1931. Others produced planning legislation later up until 2000.

In practice, planning models in Latin America exists mainly in political, social and professional discourses. They do not reflect the development process and its socio-economic dynamic and plans are no more than formal documents instead of instruments for change. Urban expansion takes place outside municipal controls led by migration and the real state market. There are few national strategies or regional policies and few municipalities, mainly big cities, have land use plans and only some are used as guides to local government actions. The mainly sectoral planning process faces financial, technical and institutional difficulties. There is a need of a new planning culture.

1.2.5   The economic waves and the effects on cities and the planning practices

The 1929 American crash terminated the cycle of prosperity based on the agro-export model. During the 1930s and the 1940s the countries were compelled to search new ways of overcoming the limitations of their rural-based economies. Some countries with an incipient industrial base started a new process in the mid 1940s substituting the imported products for internal consumption. Argentina and Brazil were pioneering new societies led by the industrial entrepreneurial sector, while in the rest of the continent the development of the industrialisation process was uneven.

This economic cycle ended in the 1960s and a new industrial model was set up open to the international market and based on neo-liberalism. In the early 1970s even the less industrialised countries, such as Bolivia, Paraguay and Ecuador, experienced significant expansion. But the combination of several factors – a weak position in the international market, the sluggish productive structures and, above all, the heavy burden of external debt brought stagnation to this positive trend by the mid 1980s.

From the 1950s the attraction of the main cities was unstoppable for migrants. The previous unitary urban morphology changed dramatically. The tensions between the private speculative forces and the public improvised actions brought about an anarchic aggregation of parts. The interest for city and regional planning emerged in the 1960s, as a result of the presence of specialised professionals. However, the few master plans drawn up at that time – Bogotá, Caracas, Rio de Janeiro, Buenos Aires - were unable to solve the existing urban problems. The absence of a legal structure to control land use, the limited technical capacity of the local administration, weak political will, lack of finance, inexistence of a regional perspective of central governments, were all obstacles to proper planning.

Mega cities

Dual cities

1.2.6 The need for external assistance

The lack of administrative capacity for planning – technical, financial and institutional – has attracted international development agencies, private organisations, NGOs and universities. External assistance has assisted in the production of local development plans in several countries like Argentina. In El Salvador plans produced by the central government are usually supported by international bilateral funding (IADB, WB). In most countries, municipal plans are also drawn up in collaboration with NGOs and foreign private institutions.

1.2.7 Some positive outcomes

Despite the great material difficulties which Latin America faces some positive outcomes were achieved:
- squatter regularisation and appropriate re-use of land
- participatory models regarding projects and budgets in some municipalities
- inclusion of planning in the political agenda as a mean to reducing the impact of natural disasters
- production of physical plans as technical tools to assist poverty reduction policies, such as in Honduras.
- experimenting with new approaches to planning
- promotion of changes in the culture of social organisation through emerging bottom-up processes
- increased role of municipalities in new legal instruments
- new instruments for planning management
- administrative promotion of plans in some important cities, regions and special areas
- plans becoming policy guides for local governments
- inclusion of participation of neighbours in democratic decision making incorporated in new planning legislation.

1.2.8   Key trends of the 21st century: globalisation and sustainability

Both aspects are affecting planning practice. Globalisation requires new ways of governing the city to take advantage of its benefits while sustainability demands new attitudes towards the way of living as a whole. This double challenging context is imposing changes and structural reforms on the countries´ administrative structures, including the traditional planning model and implementation mechanisms which were clearly unable to respond to the existing economic, social and environmental problems.

Decentralisation, governance, public participation, bottom-up approaches, empowerment, local government, regional approach, environmental policies, strategic planning, participative budgets, ministry of cities, partnership, administrative links, local agendas 21, are some of the new concepts included in the legal bodies and planning practices which were put into motion since the 1990s to overcome the past challenges.

This is the path the Latin-American countries are developing to increase their capacity as states to face the future of their cities and territories. However, changes due to globalisation and the perceived need of sustainability take different forms and intensities in different parts of the world.

The various spatial development processes sketched out here in both the developed and the developing worlds encompass the shift from the planned city to planning for cities. When comparing the orderly and bustling Greek city with the modern city in his seminal work, "The City in History", Mumford[15] states that while the city was its own world in the past, today's world has become a city. This urbanising world depends though, on contextual geo-political influences which vary widely between cities, countries and continents.

1.3 Contextual Change of Planning Since the Second World War in Europe

The contextual geo-political influences since the second world war - the period referred to in the majority of the IMPP contributions - and how planning responded to them in the developed world with focus on Europe and to some extent in North America is sketched out below, as these effects affected development processes worldwide.

1.3.1   Raising the head again: the fifties

In the fifties, decolonisation, with varying outcomes of the relationship between the colonial powers and the possessions they had to relinquish, has affected the development process of both parties. Deprived of colonial resources, the colonists had to resort to their indigenous assets to reconstruct their countries after the second world war. Conversely, after their independence, many countries were left with the planning systems they had inherited from their colonial times which may not have suited their own aspirations nor their indigenous resources. Austerity, scarcity of labour and building materials, rationing and other constraints afflicted western Europe while eastern Europe fell under communist rule and its planned economy. In theory, they presented ideal conditions for planning with all the powers and resources concentrated in the hands of a single agent, the state. In the south, planning tended to remain in the hands of the architects which produced large scale architecture and compositions devoid of socio-economic or environmental content.

1.3.2   Unique heydays: the sixties

In contrast in the sixties, possibly a unique period never to replicate again, planning enjoyed arguably the greatest influence in the development process in western Europe. No longer considered as "not-so-gifted colleagues of architects"[16], planners were expected to create an adequate setting for the new post-war society which was thriving on growth, technology and full employment. Planners were put in the driving seat of urban development and renewal, but they failed to bring the planning debate into the public realm.

The sixties underwent many short term changes. In the early sixties, planning was still carried out as if it dealt with war damage. However, dissenting voices started to denounce 'bulldozer' planning, considering it more destructive than the war itself. Student revolts were rife. They had a profound impact on the public realm and triggered the debate on 'the right to the city' led by the likes of Henri Lefebvre[17] and Manual Castells[18]. While youth in Paris in 1968 called for 'imagination au pouvoir'[19] scientists committed themselves to social responsibility[20]. Political debate increased the timelag between planning decisions and implementation. Regardless, 'pret-a-penser'[21] planning continued to operate with certainty, remained growth oriented, mesmerised by technological fixes and public sector led, while motorisation led to urban sprawl.

Postwar ubiquitous "prefab" high density urban sprawl

Postwar ubiquitous CBD

1.3.3   Crisis prone times: the seventies

The seventies were putting a stop to that. While the economy was still growing exponentially during the early seventies, dissenting voices like the Club of Rome[22] warned of the limits to growth. Through redundant NASA physicists, mathematical modelling had found its way into planning which aspired to become a science. Planning theories developed in California travelled to British universities and practices and later to continental Europe. This technocratic approach thrived during the property boom but was overtaken by the arrival of management 'science' and planning by objective in the public sector during the oil shock and the ensuing economic crisis. OPEC's quadrupling of the oil price sent tremors through the foundations of planning based on the supremacy of the motor car. Increasingly, decision makers were no longer willing to seek 'rationality' in a panacea of 'scientism' but subordinated their thinking to the computer industry. Douglas Lee's 'Requiem for large scale planning models'[23] marked another turning point away from single solutions to diversity and localism with which the post-modernists challenged the certainty of modernity later on. The post '68 reforms had bred a new generation of community activists who joined forces with the greens and got world exposure at the UN environment conference in 1972. Conservationism had colonised architectural heritage. Yet it also paved the way towards immobilism.

In the depths of the new recession, material preoccupations were once more displacing idealism in the mid-seventies, as Futuribles' longitudinal work on European values demonstrates. Thus, the plea for "shelter for all" endorsed by the 1976 UN Habitat conference in Vancouver remained unanswered. As was the demand for greater quality of the built environment and fulfilment of citizens' needs. However, ISOCARP postulated planning principles of *'idees forces'* instead of *'idees fixes'* in its own charter.[25]

1.3.4   Turbulence, divisiveness and austerity again: the eighties

In the eighties, erratic economies with widely fluctuating inflation and debt levels which politicians seemed unable to tame, together with preoccupations with the nuclear threat at the height of the cold war raised awareness of worldwide instability. Planning was confronted with unprecedented complexity which enabled other professions to enter the field. Getting into disrepute during the short lived property booms planning strove for arbitration powers between the conflicting forces which intervened in the built environment with negligible political control. With the withdrawal of the state and the reduction of the welfare state and devolution without budgets, liberalism entered large scale urban regeneration through public private partnerships as substitutes of perceived prevarication by planning.

During yet another world recession individualism and materialism were encouraged by many governments of the north as they saw a need for greater competitiveness. This strategy was challenged in 1980 by the Brandt "North-South Report"[26] reminding society of its global responsibilities. Protectionism and unshared wealth was opposed later by the Brundlandt Report[27] which, in 1987, advocated worldwide solidarity and cooperation, including on environmental protection and the problems of rapid urbanisation. While national governments were confronted globally, cities and regions, assisted by social movements were challenging national governments in turn, claiming a right to cultural identity and more independence in working towards recovery, just when planning seemed to stay in the way of development. The unexpected end of the cold war with the symbolic fall of the Berlin wall changed the perspective of the nineties. Planners were expecting unprecedented opportunities from the repercussions of world peace.

1.3.5 Hopes and disappointments: the nineties

In the nineties, the demise of communism in Eastern Europe brought with it the desire of instant satisfaction. Global capitalism was conquering the east at breathtaking speed and jeopardised planning in the handling of the peace dividend. International bodies such as NATO, CSCE, the WTO, the World Bank, other geo-political regional agencies, as well as the EU with its emerging single market had to readjust to the Asian tiger, and also to the plethora of local conflicts and genocides which triggered destruction and human displacement in an uncertain and unstable world. Eventually, the world had to cope - de facto - with the domination of a single hegemonic power and its radical fallouts. Planners had several options. They could convert themselves into negotiators between politicians, developers and the public. Others became 'footloose' planners, engaged in remedying man-made and natural disasters top down wherever they occurred. A minority preferred to become 'barefoot' planners, working directly with local communities from the bottom up.

During ever shorter and steeper boom and bust cycles, combining recession with austerity drive or stagflation, crisis management became the order of the day in a globalising world of merry-go-round mergers and turncoat acquisitions driven by opportunistic behaviour. While high unemployment was stubbornly resisting structural economic change, lasting rifts emerged in society, together with an underclass and rising fundamentalism with all its dangers of frustration, rebellion and lawlessness. Perhaps as a reaction to such turbulence, planners sought a more strategic approach to planning at Habitat II[28] and developed criteria to plan a better future for cities at URBAN 21.[29]

1.3.6 Disillusionments of the new century

Barbara Tuchman[30] showed how scientific discovery at the turn of the 19th century and social change promised prosperity and equity for the 20th century. Yet Europe, and later the whole world chose to use these assets for unprecedented destruction. Even Nicolai Kondratiev's[31] long range curves of economic change and progress were effectively linked to wars.

Just when collective memory was brushed aside as a hindrance, the seeds of a fragmented society sown during the last part of the 20th century came into their own in the early twenty hundreds. Although 'sustainability' had become a 'buzz' word at the end of the nineties, reality points rather in an opposite direction. The Kyoto agreement on green house gas emissions proved a disappointment and EU climate change objectives for the early 21st century remain far from the mark. Deregulation, liberalisation, global markets and physical as well as social segregation invite short lived quick fixes. The promising information age increases the divide between the information-poor and the information-rich, compounding other geographic and political inequalities. Such fragmentation and polarisation seems to be the price of overall relentless growth and a new challenge for planners.

1.4 Global perspective of 21st century change

The geo-politics of the early 21st century present many contradictions. They range from laudable peace and reconciliation initiatives to pre-emptive armed aggression and contested occupation, while local feuds perpetuate death, torture and rebellion in many countries throughout the world. War against terrorism becomes 'capitalism of fear'[32] leading to war on freedom and civilised ways of life. 'Poverty made history' objectives seem subjected to blanket imposition of neo-liberalism on weak economies. Brutal regimes go unscathed alongside development aid tied to capitalist self-interest. Force and corruption often have the upper hand over social justice and human rights.

At the turn of the 21st century, scientific advancements in micro-biology, genetics, communication technology and many other fields raised great expectations. Like at previous turns of centuries, scientific discovery was going to produce positive social change and widespread material wealth, notwithstanding the unknown ethical issues they raised. Yet, as early as 2001, 9/11 managed to shatter hopes of a humanistic golden age resting on eternal peace. Arbitrariness of terrorism is truly global with devastating and unjust local repercussions in cities and localities the world over, displacements, forced migration, hunger and poverty on the one hand and indecent riches on the other hand. Time may have come to revisit values and inter-cultural relations, those of the planning profession among them. Isocarp had already revisited the outcome of traditional planning when it critically examined first world and third world requirements of planners[33] and recommended:

- long term planning of the use and management of resources
- achieving planning objectives without economic growth

- improving public participation and implementation
- influencing politics through planning more adapted to the needs of the public
- nurturing robust professional ethics through on-going appraisal.

These objectives are taken up and discussed in many IMPP contributions. How well they can fare against development pressures, speed and expediency of 21st century liberalism is another matter. Despite a vivid discourse about decentralisation, democratisation and localism, public participation and transparency of the planning system find themselves marginalised. The ambiguity between participation and consultation persists, and the balance is tipping toward private development rights over the public interest in many planning systems, undermining empowerment of communities in local development affairs. Besides vocal single purpose groups which manifest against local planning proposals, protest movements seem to be confined to international concerns, such as global warming or climate change, and even those are timid compared to the street protests of the latter 20th century. A feeling of no hope in planning matters may put off civil society, withdrawing to the virtual public realm and individual private pursuits instead, a development prone to undermine the stated aim of social cohesion and equity through spatial integration. Directly relevant to planning is that land markets and property rights tend to overtake planning and sustainable development as the custodians of the public interest.

Here is not the place for a history of city planning, safe to note that planning ideas of what Benevolo calls the 'post-liberal' city involving some state intervention, have travelled to the colonies in the past and have spread worldwide in the 20th century with the modern and post-modern movements. IMPP evidence illustrates how these regulatory ideas are used at present, who is in charge of implementing them, and how this process varies widely between different cultures.

1.5   Where does that leave planners?

The best planning system and the most competent planners are not sheltered from geo-political changes which are influencing the development process beyond their reach. What characterises physical development regardless of who initiates it, is that it brings about change. This raises the issue of the legitimacy of planning as well as of those who carry it out. Individuals, social group, all sorts of 'lay' planners were all involved over time, as were their masters or political representatives, surveyors and technical experts; and when the development system became more formalised professional land-use planners,[34] spatial planners, strategic planners, comprehensive planners, regional planners, advocacy planners, community planners, specialist planners, interactive planners, mediating planners... During times of relative certainty, planners and architects were in an unchallenged position to plan and those in the public sector to implement plans. However, the widespread diversity of spatial development conditions reflected in the IMPP contributions has clearly changed this situation and planning is often seen at a crossroads or powerless.

What role, if any, are planners to play? There is little chance of them becoming the sole genitor of the public interest, nor to command the authority of arbiter between conflicting interests with so much at stake outside democratic control. Yet, even more than the demise of the cold war, the effects of post cold war hegemony could provide planning with a new lease of life and tasks beyond current thinking.

2 | Trends of Planning, Implementation and Development
Lessons learnt from the planning experience of 101 countries

From the outside, the development process - and planning in particular - is sometimes perceived as an inherent act of destruction in the interplay between perceived socio-political 'progress' and spatial development. It has first to eliminate what there is — be it wilderness or man-made landscapes, existing buildings or infrastructure - to replace it with new physical solutions in response to demands of society or specific interests. Yet, more often than not, such drastic and resource squandering action fails to satisfy the expectations of a changing and increasingly affluent society. It could be argued that any intervention in physical space, be it direct action in a given situation, or measures taken according to plans devised by planners for the planned, is similarly disruptive. From such a standpoint, there is no essential difference between a masterminded, approved development and spontaneous informal settlements which spring up out of sheer necessity. This argument is at the heart of the evidence which the IMPP has brought together.

Ubiquitous informal settlements

Ubiquitous suburban sprawl

No attempt is made here to synthesise the vast and rich material presented in the IMPP. The purpose is to illustrate the key issues which were addressed in most countries. They are grouped into interdependent categories which, together constitute the major preoccupations of to-day's planning practice. The selected findings are based on regional comparisons. They highlight similarities and singularities across continents grouped into nine interdependent areas: governance; national planning framework, plan making and decisions; regionalisation; public participation; sharing planning powers; implementation problems; lack of planning skills; environment - ecology – sustainability; and design issues. They inspire some conclusions on the state of the current art of planning, future prospects and implication for the planning profession.

2.1.1 Governance

Governance is recognised as a crucial factor in the success or failure of the planning process. Political ambitions often entail short term preferences and over-ambitious projects, resulting in disillusionment of the key players in the development industry, as well as scepticism among the general public. The transition from government, with its traditional hierarchy, sectoral segregation, lack of transparency, poor internal communication, and sometimes authoritarian character, opacity in financing and outright corruption, to governance which promises subsidiarity, devolution including of tax raising powers, horizontal and vertical cooperation and coordination, and empowerment of the citizenry with effective participation is far from being achieved. Considering the wide variety of cultural and historic conditions, size and economy of countries, there is no optimum amount of levels of governance and no consensus about which lowest tier is best. Neither is there a single model for bottom up or top down decision making or any combination of the two, the latter being advocated in various forms but rarely achieved. Nor is there an optimum relationship between political powers, professional input which includes planners and fiscal status at any level of governance. A particular issue is governance of the public realm, including how to share responsibilities for national parks and other communal assets, and particularly those which assist sustainability in the longer term.

These issues affect the workings of the planning system directly and development potential indirectly. They were often singled out in the IMPP contributions as in need of change, considering that the planning system tends to mirror government structure with the same deficiencies.

2.1.2   National planning framework, plan making and decisions

Many contributions revealed very complex but also too general and vague planning systems and overcomplicated related administrative structures. In many cases, and in particular in poorer countries there is little relationship between these complex planning systems, often inherited from colonial times, the needs of people at various levels, and the development process in general which takes place in reality. There also exist contradictions or lack of coordination between spatial and sectoral national plans.

Hierarchic systems often include a national land use plan. This affects the workings of the planning hierarchy and the contributions of each part of it, and not always in a positive manner. It tends to slow down both the decision making and the plan making process which in many countries replicates existing formulae and trends, instead of being pro-active or forward looking. In case of complex planning instruments and guidelines they tend to be ignored. Thus many plans are never produced despite time horizons laid down by legislation. For lack of political will there is little connection between planning objectives and decisions regarding spatial interventions either by the public or more often by the private sector. Often medium and long term national development strategies are missing or give way to short term, politically motivated interventions.

However, some countries use national land use plans as a general instrument for land and financial allocation throughout space and the hierarchic system of governance. Sometimes national land use plans replace past economic five year plans. Also, some countries have successfully introduced strategic planning at regional level and city level, most of the time initiated by these levels themselves. Part of their success was that they avoided precise land use designation, leaving room of manoeuvre for practical development proposals.

2.1.3   Regionalisation

Planning is increasingly challenged by the tension between corporate private or public power and the aspirations of civil society; between globalism and its counterproductive gigantism, and localism and its 'nimby' myopia. Modern planning systems propose a tripartite integrative structure to deal with these contradictions, resorting to regions as a mediating level between localism and large scale national and international development pressures.

Governance led regionalisation was expected to redress the traditional weakness of the intermediary level or levels of government between the nation state and the lowest tier of communities. Often, levels in between were at the intersection of the arm of the state and local, albeit rarely self-governing administrations. Moreover, they shared few areas of responsibilities and were often excluded from spatial planning.

The rise of the cities and their increasing importance in the global economy had repercussions on both national governance and local development levels. Central authorities perceived them as potential threats, to the extend that inter-governmental organisations started to focus on cities.[35] With increasing international competition, cities broadened their influence by forming networks with neighbouring cities and constituting strategic entities at regional level, often in the absence of any corresponding statutory structure. Many recent issues, protection of nature and agricultural land, climate change and sustainability among them, joined traditional tools of competitiveness such as transportation connections or sharing of capital intensive infrastructures of energy supply or waste disposal. Regions were considered the best level to deal with these large scale undertakings, especially during privatisation of utilities and other public sector infrastructure which endured gradual withdrawal of the state in infrastructure investment.

Regionalisation is intimately linked with new forms of governance, often in need of being invented altogether. Even in small island countries, regions were adopted as an intermediary scale between local and national perspectives with focus on socio-economic matters. New regionalism meant a dynamic and innovative climate of cooperation and power sharing. France, a traditionally centralised country, for example, has pioneered new flexible forms of negotiated cooperation at large regional scale.

Conversely, regions have been instated in large countries in the developing world, such as Argentina which have no real practical roles, let alone powers and resources. The very large scale super-regions of the United States, mainly in populated areas on the east and west coasts, as

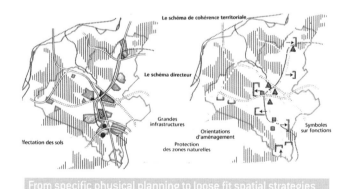

Le schéma de cohérence territoriale

Le schéma directeur

Grandes infrastructures

Orientations d'aménagement

Protection des zones naturelles

ffectation des sols

Symboles sur fonctions

From specific physical planning to loose fit spatial strategies

well as in Texas are preparing the ground for a national plan, an interesting concept in a liberal and federal country. In Europe, what started as 'the blue banana', encompassing the richest parts of the north west, has become the pentagon including London, Paris, Brussels, Frankfurt and Milan. Together with their polycentric city systems it is considered sole capable of competing in the global economy. The concept of the southern European Diagonal[37] in the faster growing region of Europe, branching out to Latin America, North Africa and eastern Europe is the latest addition to such large scale regional concepts for strategic planning and development.

In other areas, regionalisation has extended further into complete separation, such as the now independent republics of ex-Yugoslavia. Pressures for such devolution exist in many countries where social, cultural and/or religious cohesion is lacking: Sudan or Nigeria in Africa, Iraq and Israel in the Middle East and many others. Other countries are experiencing continuous pressures for such devolution or complete separation, Scotland, Wales and Northern Ireland in the UK, the Flemish, Walloon regions and Brussels in Belgium, the Basque country and Catalonia in Spain, many de facto divided island states, such as Cyprus and Sri Lanka. These situations are clearly reflected in the IMPP contributions and in each case, planning is directly affected, as it is often being carried out with great independence in the various parts of these countries. Issues raised are whether such divisions are prone to creating greater economic and social polarisation between various parts of countries, thus running counter to the traditional objective of spatial strategic and regional planning, namely redressing disparities and assisting more equitable development. This incidentally is the stated aim of the ESDP (European Spatial Development Perspective)[38] which polycentrism is expected to achieve.

2.1.4   Public participation

Public participation is either compulsorily incorporated, encouraged in planning legislation or omitted altogether, and many IMPP contributions consider that public participation is wanting. Countries with liberal economies tend to state that participation hampers the development process without contributing anything in return. The bottom up perspective claims greater empowerment. In some and often more deprived countries there exist explicit budgets, mechanisms and encouragements for participation. In poor and very poor countries such 'participation' takes a direct form and manifests itself as informal settlement development, often on illegally occupied land. In practice the greatest urban developers are the self-builders. While making a vital contribution to shelter provision this leads to considerable contradictions with the planning system. Nevertheless, the informal urbanisation process is sometimes allowed by laws under certain circumstances.

Conversely, participation is interpreted as the right of land owners to form part of the planning process. In countries where public participation is incorporated in the statutory planning system, albeit often emaciated into public consultation, it is felt to offer too little too late. This tends to result in apathy and a feeling of powerlessness, which may manifest itself in demonstrations against large scale, often state led interventions. The issue of corruption forms part of this debate, undermining democratic planning, citizen empowerment and participation. Some countries make a concerted effort in pro-active top down consultation. This is often the case after recent independence. Contradictory conventional wisdom sees the merits of participation as the means to make decisions stick on the one hand, and as expensive delay without benefits on the other hand.

2.1.5   Sharing planning powers

The three issues of governance, regionalisation and public participation are all connected with power sharing. The private sector has become an increasingly important partner in the planning process. Most countries, even those with some form of social state system are adopting market practises in physical development, more recently in Lybia, Egypt or Mozambique. Regardless whether land remains in the hands of the collectivity, the state, the local authorities, or an autocratic ruler, the private sector is the major player in implementing physical development, either on its own, or in partnership with the public sector. Privatisation, decentralisation, withdrawal of state funding are common to many countries and a large variety of partnerships has found its way into planning legislation or practice. Even the public sector, cities, clusters of cities and regions, have developed institutions which enable them to operate more freely in the market and become a substantial enabler, guarantor, lender or investor and risk sharer in large scale, long term development projects. They consist of mainly infrastructure with real estate spin offs for the private sector. What this means for mainstream planning is that it can be bypassed by development corporations and similar agencies set up to kick start and accelerate the development process. Waterfront developments on displaced ports are a common example throughout the world.

The experience of countries which achieved independence with the demise of the Soviet Union is relevant here. State planned economy in total control of implementation should have provided the best possible planning results. After adjustment of planning and especially land and property rights to the market economy, the free for all era required an early return to control mechanism, sometimes restructuring those which had remained on the statute books. Similar effects are observed in countries which shed their influence of communism, many of them in the developing world, while undergoing unplanned and unprecedented adverse effects during rapid expansion of the real estate sector.

Power sharing, or complaints about its absence, are also occurring between the various levels and sectors of planning. Several models live alongside each other, top down strictly controlled planning systems which use lower tiers of planning mainly to implement national strategies. More rarely, systems work from the bottom up, based on self governing communities, often tribal or rural organisations. Together, they constitute cumulative development processes, however seldom without some national strategy, except in most federal countries.

Absence of power sharing leads to ambiguities and overlaps between competences of various levels and sectors, mentioned by many countries as serious hindrances of the efficient working of the planning system. Sometimes, sectors at the national level, such as water management, coastal protection, or defence arrangements overrule any arrangements at lower tiers. Conversely, in certain circumstances there is no clarity about responsibilities and powers, for example in the case of natural disasters or wars. Conflicts exist also at the macro level, mainly between the planning system and the economy, and sometimes with environmental strategies or even social objectives. The latter tend to appear in countries with distinct social groups and aboriginal people.

Many countries made a concerted effort at decentralisation, sometimes contrived by outside forces, in the case of financial assistance or hope to join international groupings. Often centralisation prevails in reality owing to lack of local finance or political legitimacy. Rare exceptions, such as in some Latin American countries have introduced genuine bottom up spatial management initiatives in their new governance structures. There is also an issue of administrative reality which often does not follow spatial development, such as in metropolitan areas which have no effective tool of integrated spatial management.

2.1.6   Implementation problems

All the preceding aspects find repercussions in implementation. In a number of countries, planning tends to become an aim in itself, distinct from any implementation programmes, even from any possibility of ever being implemented. Lack of finance, technical expertise, sometimes land, sometimes political will are all invoked as reasons for preventing implementation. In most countries, the private sector, which includes crucially landowners, is the major player in implementation. Legislation in quite a few countries explicitly enables the private sector to take an active part in planning. Areas which it proposes for development would be exempt from the plans in operation and would give rise to amendments or new plans altogether. It does not follow though that such sites will be developed and this preoccupies some countries, especially those where the public sector does not own land, nor benefit from adequate planning powers.

Quite a number of countries voiced concerns about the effectiveness of the planning systems in operation as they were complex, time and money consuming, suffered from duplication and vacuums, or outright obstructions. Improvisation was rife, the system lacked expert inputs, and thus had no chance of leading to implementation. A main reason was that the planning process tended to lag behind requirements of the economy and plan updating was poor and lacked assessment of results, feedback and monitoring. In places like Nigeria there is no attempt to relate the planning system to reality or to control over what is being built. Many other reasons hamper implementation, among them frequently changing administrative structures, lack of social legitimacy, insufficient local authority powers and finance, or political support and continuity. Such administrations are tolerating lapses of both public and private sector planning obligations. Sometimes enforcement instruments are weak or non existent which prevents planning authorities from coping with illegal use of land and buildings. However, no country proposed to abolish the planning system altogether.

2.1.7   Lack of planning skills

Upholding the planning system does not mean that awareness of the fallacies of the planning system was poor. The most urgent obstacle to planning was considered the lack of technical knowledge and know how, infrastructure, equipment, databases and above all education. Many countries showed explicit interest in improving planning education and setting it up, especially in developing countries, where only the richest administrations were able to obtain support from external consultants. Planning education was also advocated for politicians, civil servants and civil society at large. Similarly, lack of research and research infrastructure was deplored and seen as a cause for brain drain and loss of the best indigenous planners.

2.1.8   Environment - ecology - sustainability

For a long time physical planning was at the centre, if not alone in proposing and regulating physical development in cities and in the countryside. With increasing awareness of environmental impacts of rapid urbanisation, better knowledge of ecological consequences of development, and more recently the preoccupation with sustainability physical planning had to share its field with environmental concerns. In countries like Sweden and the Netherlands, environmental planning formed an equal second pillar with physical spatial planning. In New Zealand, environmental concerns are the sole determinant of spatial development regulation. All countries in Latin America have approved specific legislation for the preservation of their natural resources. A sustainable vision was included in most countries as a key instrument to bridge the gap between planning legislation and physical development.

Increasingly, some convergence between the objectives of spatial development and environmental protection can be found in single planning documents. Many issues remain outstanding, such as definition, measurement, and prediction of long term effects of the spatial development process on the environment, the economy and society. The short term horizon of political decision making tends to act against longer term investigations and monitoring. This dilemma constitutes the full circle of the main issues discussed in connection with physical and spatial planning in the IMPP contributions.

2.1.9   Design issues

One last word though. Although planning has a tradition of large scale architecture and design in many countries, especially in the south, it has moved into more abstract spheres, incorporating economic, social and environmental considerations and leaving design itself to those in charge of implementation. This provoked reactions in some countries where, especially those entrusted with development control found that they did not have the tools to secure high quality design of development proposals, often put together by financiers, the real estate sector or the construction industry.

Some movements originated outside planning which put pressure on governments and planning institutions to attach greater importance to quality of design and quality of life when designing and building new developments, or regenerating existing physical environments. New urbanism is such a movement. Yet overall, aesthetics and quality of design are holding a relatively small part in the IMPP contributions. Nevertheless, there is recognition of the need for a high quality public realm to make developments liveable, and thus profitable.

2.2 Challenges for the planning process

The many and often comprehensive contributions to the IMPP provide a unique opportunity to explore the challenges encountered by planning processes. Due to their inherent inertia planning systems tend to be inadequate in responding to a fast changing world and in adjusting the existing physical reality to new requirements. On the whole, political structures and corresponding regulatory powers are still geared toward devising formal, legalistic development strategies. However, with shrinking public resources, their implementation depends increasingly on market mechanisms and the private sector. Driven by land markets and actions of land owners, investors and developers - the key agents of the development industry – substantial physical development tends to occur outside exclusive or direct control of the public sector. Conversely, development in shrinking cities is not forthcoming despite plans. Clearly, the relationship between planning authorities and the development industry requires adjustment. In particular, new forms of governance have to be invented with the capacity of mediating and negotiating between an ever more complex array of actors.

Over and above institutional adjustments required at national, regional and local levels, new planning issues emerge from geo-political concerns, such as sustainability, climate change, biodiversity, scarcity of resources and, most relevant to physical planning, better husbandry of land and the existing built and natural environment.

Civil society is exercising pressures in many places to overcome the democratic deficit of decision making on physical change at the local level. Expressions of greater public involvement range from stultifying 'nimbyism' to innovative forms of community action. At the other end of the spectrum, the need to conceive a broader, longer term perspective of strategic spatial development manifests itself at an ever growing scale, both in the context of rapid urbanisation and economic decline. The most promising development concepts devised at city and metropolitan levels extend to regional levels, and in some cases they even produce supra-national, longer term spatial visions, such as America 2025 in a large federal state,[39] the ESDP in Europe hatched initially by a handful of planners[40] encouraged by some enlightened ministers, or the Southern European Diagonal.[41] In turn, these large scale spatial strategies require new forms of cooperation between competing economic power bases, essentially cities and city regions, motivating them to seek complementary functions instead of engaging in debilitating competition between them when facing global survival.

All these recent developments have repercussions on the planning profession. As evidenced in the IMPP contributions, it voices its own preoccupations about its knowledge base and the learning process required to equip planners with appropriate instruments in dealing with the many predicted, but also the often unforeseeable issues arising in an increasingly volatile world.

3 | **Conclusions**

3.1 Implications for the future of planning and the planning profession

The discussion of the IMPP material reveals that essential planning challenges raised are all interrelated and interconnected. This reflects the complex, maybe impossible nature of the tasks facing both politicians and planners alike. Yet, it has to be recognised that planning cannot hope to resolve the whole gamut of economic, environmental and social problems, although governments believe that reforms may bring about solutions. In reality, these constant changes make life very difficult for those bodies and agencies, both public and private, which have to 'plan' their medium-term investment strategies.

3.1.1   Professional expertise

Planners are facing a three pronged future. They are expected to imagine visions at an increasingly broader and long term scale, but also to find instant solutions to specific demands, and all the while to adjust to a planning system in continuous flux. As pointed out in many IMPP contributions, planners face a paraphernalia of related problems, such as the lack of appropriate analytical methodologies, inadequate data, and ways of keeping abreast with fast evolving planning technology, besides the need to define the limits of control and influence.[42] The complex world in which planners have to operate leaves precious little time for intellectual and professional regeneration. Conventional wisdom continues to postulate that the timescale of reflection and analysis is incompatible with the pressing nature of planning problems and the short term time horizon of politics. Not surprisingly, planning is poorly backed by science and research.

3.1.2   Planning education

Planning is a vocational profession and cannot rest on academic education alone. It has to rely on learning by doing. However, widespread pressures to accelerate the planning process are reducing time for knowledge exchange and interaction in practice and may lead to deskilling planners while discouraging newcomers to the profession. The rapid and profound changes which affect the tasks of planners require continuous upgrading of their knowledge and know how. Deficiencies and inadequacies of planning education were noted in most developing countries, but also elsewhere. There is a clear need of pooling resources and the planning knowledge base and the new edition of IMPP attempts to make some contribution towards this aim. Learning from experience and best practice elsewhere has its limitations, but many planning issues are shared widely and transfer of lessons learnt from experiments are invaluable in a world more conscious of having to manage with limited resources. This leaves the question of who should learn and train about planning besides the professionals: politicians, administrators, developers and civil society?

3.1.3   Future role of planners and the planning profession

Even in the eyes of the most adamant subscribers to the free market, some regulation is indispensable for the smooth running of the built environment and its development. The question is who is providing and implementing the regulatory process on whose behalf. Planners are included in greater accountability claimed by civil society and need to revisit their role as well as their skills. Many suggestions are put forward in the IMPP contributions, not least a more solid knowledge base and greater self reliance of the planned. A more discerned use of borrowed knowledge and the need to change the image of planning and planners are recurrent themes.

Cities for people

3.2 Globalisation, development and planning

Development processes have become very dynamic in the globalising world. Thus countries are seeking new approaches to accommodate economic and social change while managing their spatial and environmental repercussions in a widely varying context, ranging from advanced, emerging to stagnating economies. Akin to trans-national concentrations of corporate economic actors in response to globalisation, it is in the interest of nation states to undertake joint efforts at coordinating certain policies at supra-national scale. Often this implies a national vision of spatial development, not as a static plan but as a flexible strategy, a framework for grasping opportunities and action.

In the globalising economy, cities have become the main drivers of economic growth and social progress and find themselves at the forefront of socio-economic impacts on their physical fabric. Their planning powers put them in charge of spatial organisation and sustainable management while preserving architectural heritage, the natural environment and, most importantly, urbanity in a competitive environment. In the exercise of these powers they are facing the difficult task of balancing public and private interests when allocating land and user rights in both fast developing and shrinking situations. In this process, cities have reinforced their pro-active role, acquired new skills of city marketing while often becoming themselves commercial partners in the development process. Aware that investment is seeking competitive locations resilient to adverse effects of globalisation, cities realised that it was to their advantage to offer wider opportunities with greater variety to inward and especially international investment.

By coordinating certain spatial strategies at a broader scale cities are able to cooperate beyond their boundaries in networked projects by pooling complementary city assets. The 'urban project', 'projet urbain' as French planners coin it, has become the 'region project',[43] a means for regions to move centre stage. Such up-scaling is a noticeable trend, but with cooperation at increasing spatial scale demands for greater local autonomy and self-reliance at community level are becoming more pressing. In a number of countries creative initiatives occur at the lowest level and work themselves up through the planning system into spatial policies. These developments hint at a new urban and perhaps a new planning culture.

The innovative approaches to spatial strategies at all these levels have repercussions on the planning system. What emerges from the IMPP evidence is a "horses for courses" outcome as each country attempts to establish a system of governance and planning which reflects its particular political imperatives and cultural ethos.

The planning system like all dynamic changes in the globalising world has to innovate and adjust through better use of existing resources and diversification. The top down, chain of command physical planning system seems on its way out, or remaining merely as a relic 'exercise in style' without even attempting any consequences on the real world. Alternative operational approaches, such as para-public development corporations, often run by retired generals at arms length but ultimately under control of the state to accelerate the development process show signs of being replaced by more inclusive instruments of implementation involving a broad spectrum of key actors directly who ultimately realise development or refrain from objection. The evaluations of the IMPP contributions point clearly to a new era beyond formal judicial planning, more flexible, operational, responsive to outside threats and opportunities, involving key actors and civil society as of right to constantly rebalance the right and aspirations of individuals with the public good.

NOTES

1. Judith Ryser, Waikeen Ng (ed). 2005. Four Decades of Knowledge Creation and Sharing. ISOCARP and Fundacion Metropoli.
2. Karl Polanyi. 1957. The Great Transformation, the political and economic origins of our time. Beacon Hill Press.
3. Leonardo Benevolo. 1980. The History of Cities. Scolar Press. First published in 1975 as Storia Della Citta, by Editori Laterza.
4. For example the Mesopotamian city of Arbela continuously inhabited for 5000 years (Benevolo op.cit p 27).
5. Richard Sennett. 1994. Flesh and Stone. The body and the city in Western civilisation. Faber and Faber.
6. Peter Hall. Cities in Civilisation. 1998. Weidenfeld and Nicholson.
7. After the utopian designs of, for example, Ledoux, Lequeue in the 18th century, Tony Garnier's Industrial City near Lyon - 1900, Charles Fourier's Phalanstere, Jean-Baptiste Godin's Familiastere, or Robert Owen's ideal village and New Lanark, or Titus Salt's Saltaire, George Cadbury's Bourneville and WH Lever's Port Sunlight, the French Planning Treatise of 1928 started the zoning idea (from Benevolo 1967/1980. op.cit)
8. Robert Owen defined town planning as follows: "to come to an arrangement which is advantageous to everyone, within a system which will permit continued and unlimited technical improvement". In: Benevolo, Leonardo.1967. The Origins of Modern Town Planning. Routledge Kegan Paul. Le Origini Dell'Urbanistica Moderna. 1963. Editori Laterza. p xiv.
9. Congres International de l'Architecture Moderne. International Congresses of Modern Architecture.
10. Athens Charter. Drafted at the 4th CIAM in Athens in 1933 and edited and publicised by Le Corbusier in 1941. It laid down the deeds of good architectural practice and the principles of the functional city.
11. European Council of Town Planners. 2003. The New Charter of Athens 2003. The European Council of Town Planners' Vision for Cities in the 21st Century. Lisbon.
12. CEHOPU. 1989. El sueño de un Orden. Ministerio de Obras Públicas y Urbanismo, Spain.
13. Martín Lou, A; Bensayasag, E; Franchini, T., 1992: Proceso de urbanización en América del Sur.Modelos de ocupacion del espacio. Colecciones Mapfre, Spain.
14. Based on IMPP entries.
15. Lewis Mumford. 1961. The City in History. Penguin (1990).
16. Sam van Embden. Some reflections on my state of the profession of 1969. In ISOCARP 25th anniversary, p 39.
17. Henri Lefebvre. 1968. Anthropos. Henri Lefebvre. 1968. Espaces et politique, le droit a la ville II. Anthropos.
18. Manuel Castells. 1968. La qestion urbaine. Maspero.
19. 'power to imagination'
20. David Rose led one such movement at the London School of Economics and Political Sciences.
21. 'ready to think'
22. Donella H Meadows, Dennis L Meadows; Jorgen Randers; William W Behrens. 1972. The Limits to Growth., a report for the Club of Rome project on the predicament of mankind. Earth Island, London.
23. Douglas Lee. 1973. Requiem for large scale planning models. In: The Journal of the American Institute of Planners.
24. Futuribles, analyse et prospective. L'evolution des valeurs des Europeens, numero special 200. July/August 1995.
25. Idees forces, ideas of strength, instead of idees fixes;, rigid ideas, conceived by Derek Lyddon.
26. Commission on International Development Issues, led by Willy Brandt. 1980. A Programme for Survival.
27. World Commission on Environment and Development, led by Gro Harlem Brundtland. 1987. Our Common Future.
28. UN Habitat Conference II. 1996. Professional and Researchers Forum. Istanbul
29. Peter Hall, Ulrich Pfeiffer (eds). 2000. URBAN 21. Global conference on the city. Berlin 2000.
30. Barbara Tuchman. 1966. The Proud Tower. Macmillan
31. Nicolai Kondratiev. 1925. The major economic cycles. Institute for Business Cycle Research. Moscow
32. Denis Duclos. Terroristes ou Citoyens. Ces industries florissantes de la peur permanente. In: Le Monde Diplomatique, aout 2005. No 617, pp 16-17.
33. ISOCARP. 1990. 25th anniversary pamphlet. ISOCARP archives.
34. The Town Planning Institute was founded in 1913 in Britain and gradually broadened the concept of planning.
35. The OECD undertook several studies on cities and governance. E.g. What policies for Globalising Cities? Rethinking the urban policy agenda. Madrid. 2007.
36. Armand B Peschard-Sverdrup. 2007. North American Future 2025 Project. CSIS (Centre for Strategic and International Studies).
37. Judith Ryser (ed). 2008. Building the European Diagonal. Fundacion Metropoli.
38. ESDP: European Spatial Developement Perspective commissioned by the Ministers of Spatial Planning of the Counsel of Europe and adopted de facto by the European Union as a tool for allocating structural funds.
39. Regional Plan Association. 2008. America 2025.
40. Andreas Faludi (ed). 2002. European Spatial Planning. Lincoln Institute of Land Use.
41. Initiated by innovative operators in the built environment like the Fundacion Metropoli in Madrid, Spain.
42. The UK Development Plan Manual produced in the 1970s already highlights the limited role of land use planning with the warning caveat "subject to the exercise of planning control and influence".
43. 'projet d'amenagement et de developpement durable' according to the new approach of SCOT: Schema de coherence territorial.

Planning systems at a glance

AFRICA

NORTH AFRICA
Algeria
Egypt
Lybia
Morocco
Tunisia

SUB-SAHARAN AFRICA
Angola
Botswana
Ghana
Kenya
Lesotho
Malawi
Namibia
Nigeria
South Africa
Sudan
Swaziland
Tanzania
Zambia
Zimbabwe

AMERICAS

NORTH AMERICA
Canada
Mexico
USA

CENTRAL AMERICA
Barbados
Costa Rica
El Salvador
Guatemala
Honduras
Trinidad and Tobago

SOUTH AMERICA
Argentina
Bolivia
Brazil
Chile
Colombia
Guyana
Paraguay
Peru
Uruguay
Venezuela

ASIA & PACIFIC

MIDDLE EAST
Iraq
Iran
Israel
Saudi Arabia

CENTRAL ASIA
Bangladesh
India
Kazakhstan
Maldivas
Pakistan
Sri Lanka
Uzbekistan

EAST ASIA
China
Hong Kong
Indonesia
Japan
Philippines
Singapore
South Korea
Taiwan
Vietnam

AUSTRALASIA & PACIFIC
Australia
New Zealand
Samoa

EUROPE

EUROPEAN UNION
Austria
Belgium
Bulgaria
Cyprus
Czech Republic
Denmark
Estonia
Finland
France
Germany
Greece
Hungary
Ireland
Italy
Latvia
Lithuania
Luxembourg
Malta
Netherlands
Poland
Portugal
Slovakia
Slovenia
Spain
Sweden
United Kingdom

EUROPEAN ECONOMIC AREA AND BILATERAL
Iceland
Norway
Switzerland

NON EUROPEAN UNION
Albania
Armenia
Azerbaijan
Bosnia
Croatia
Georgia
Kosovo
Macedonia
Russia
Serbia
Turkey

Africa

NORTH AFRICA
Algeria
Egypt
Lybia
Morocco
Tunisia

SUB-SAHARAN AFRICA
Angola
Botswana
Ghana
Kenya
Lesotho
Malawi
Namibia
Nigeria
South Africa
Sudan
Swaziland
Tanzania
Zambia
Zimbabwe

ALGERIA

FAST FACTS

- **Total Area:** 2,381,740 km²
- **Total Population:** 33,769,669
- **Population Growth:** 1.209%
- **Unemployment Rate:** 14.1%
- **GDP:** $268.9 billion
- **GDP per capita:** $8,100
- **GDP growth rate:** 4.6%

SETTLEMENTS STRUCTURE

- **Capital City:** Algiers
  1,742,800 pop
  3,917,000 (metro. area)
- **Second City:** Oran
  752,200 pop
- **Density:** 14 pop/km²
- **Urban Population:** 60%

Political and administrative organisation
People's Democratic Republic. Presidential regime. The Republic is composed of 9 regions, 48 provinces (wilaya), 553 districts (diara) and 1541 municipalities.

Administrative competence for planning
The state is responsible for the national and the regional plans; the wilaya are competent for the provincial plans and inter-communal arrangements. The municipalities are responsible for drawing up their own plans, including detail plans.

Main planning legislation
In the absence of a formal planning act (under preparation), a number of complementary regulations determine national, regional and local plan making and implementation. They are the Framework Legislation for National Spatial Planning 1987, and the Land Use Planning Regulations 1990.

Planning and implementation instruments
The planning system is hierarchical with requirement of vertical compatibility between plans.
SNAT: national spatial plan
SRAT: regional spatial plan grouping some 9 wilayas
PAW: structure plan for wilayas
PDAU: municipal or inter-municipal structure and development plan with a long term horizon, compulsory for all 1541 communes, lying down the strategies for urban extension and development
POS: municipal land use plan, required to be compatible with PDAU, determining COS, CES, formal design and building rules, prepared by professionals
Land subdivision can be initiated by developers.

Development control
Land subdivision, building and demolition permits are the responsibility of the municipalities.

Planning system in practice
There is a lack of compatibility between different levels of planning despite legal requirements. This is partly due to an uneven data base and lack of coordinating procedures. Other deficiencies include lack of consultation and insufficient technical competence of decision makers and administrators. Weak instruments of implementation and the lengthy process of plan making and approval require frequent plan revision. Also there is little coordination between socio-economic development plans and spatial strategies.

Read on: www.mhu.gov.dz; http://63.70.212.91/; www.algeria-market.com; www.univ-constantine-dz; www.ceneap.com.dz

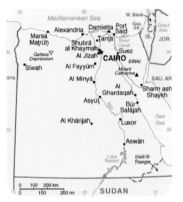

FAST FACTS

- **Total Area:** 1,001,450 km²
- **Total Population:** 81,713,517
- **Population Growth:** 1.682%
- **Unemployment Rate:** 10.1%
- **GDP:** $431.9 billion
- **GDP per capita:** $5,400
- **GDP growth rate:** 7.2%

SETTLEMENTS STRUCTURE

- **Capital City:** Cairo
  7,629,866 pop
  11,146,000 (metro. area)
- **Second City:** Alexandria
  3,891,000 pop
- **Density:** 82 pop/km²
- **Urban Population:** 42%

Political and administrative organisation

Republic composed of 26 governorates (muhafazat), regions (markazes), city administrations and municipalities.

Administrative competence for planning

The main institutions with competence for planning are the State (Ministry of Housing, Utilities and Urban Communities), General Organisation for Physical Planning (GOPP), Central Authority for Development, New Urban Communities Authority regulating new towns; national agencies responsible for utilities; 7 planning regions established in 1977 (under auspices of governorates); 188 city administrations mainly in the Nile delta; 808 rural local councils, 4329 villages mainly along the Nile.

Main planning legislation

The National Five Year Plan provides the framework for spatial planning.

Planning and implementation instruments

National 5 year plans are drawn up with economic, social and spatial targets (the fifth plan covers 2008-2013). The national spatial development strategy aims to develop desert areas and to upgrade existing urban areas. Strategic spatial development plans have a 2017 time horizon. They include 40 new towns; master plans and land use plans for 40 cities according to the 5 year plan. Since 1983 there are long term and master plans, as well as private sector operational plans for the Cairo city region and elsewhere. Detailed plans include densities and municipal service programmes.

Development control

Building regulations are applied by the cities and the rural councils. GOOP is in charge of upgrading informal areas. Historic conservation is the responsibility of cities, together with executive agencies in Cairo, Alexandria, and other large cities.

Planning system in practice

Large population growth and large migration from rural to urban areas are finding their expression in informal settlements on the fringe of cities as well as in inner city overcrowding. Top down central planning together with gated towns built entirely by private developers may not resolve the urbanisation process and especially the housing need. Moreover, the erosion of fertile land along the Nile which is invaded by urbanisation is contributing to environmental deterioration and ecological problems.

Read on: http://www.hbrc.edu.eg; http://net.shams.edu.eg;
http://www.sea1917.org

FAST FACTS

- **Total Area:** 1,759,450 km²
- **Total Population:** 6,173,579
- **Population Growth:** 2.216%
- **Unemployment Rate:** 30%
- **GDP:** $78.79 billion
- **GDP per capita:** $13,100
- **GDP growth rate:** 5.4%

SETTLEMENTS STRUCTURE

- **Capital City:** Tripoli
  1,269,700 pop
  2,357,800 (metro. area)
- **Second City:** Benghazi
  734,900 pop
- **Density:** 3.5 pop/km²
- **Urban Population:** 87%

Political and administrative organisation
The Great Socialist People's Libyan Arab Republic is composed of 4 regions and 40 municipalities (sha'biyah) which replaced the baladyiat (32) system, in turn replacing the old 3 governat system.

Administrative competence for planning
In 1964 the Urban Planning Authority was established which is in charge of long term spatial plans with targets laid down in ten year plans (1965-85; 1985-2005; 2005-25). It is the main authority responsible for regional plans. Municipalities are in charge of local master plans (land use plans) and detail plans (layouts of new urban areas).

Main planning legislation
Lybia's tradition of planning is recent and urban planning was instated after a severe earthquake in the city of El Marj in the east of the country. The 1964 legislation established the Urban Planning Authority. Planning legislation is supporting national development standards.

Planning and implementation instruments
Planning consists of a long term future oriented problem solving process, by means of national spatial programmes with a twenty to twenty five year time horizon. The planning system is hierarchic with upper level plans guiding lower level planning processes. Spatial plans include the national physical perspective plan (NPPP), regional plans (RP), master plans (MP), and layout plans (LP).

Development control
Local authorities issue building licenses based on clearly laid down standards and building regulations.

Planning system in practice
The top down sequential approach to planning is considered to work well in Lybia. It applies mainly to urbanised areas though which are relatively small considering the vast areas of desert. Cities and urban settlements are mainly located along the coast, with the bulk of urbanisation happening in and around the capital Tripoli, while oil exploration and extraction and related activities are taking place in remote areas where settlements and human activities are based on ways of life rooted in history. Nevertheless, economic activities and export strategies are having a considerable impact on the social, economic and physical structures of the regions concerned. Regional development strategies are addressing these transformations in regional spatial strategies which aim to improve living standards equally throughout the country. More recently, Lybia has started to adopt gradually some free market principles and this is bound to have repercussions on the planning system and the practices which are aimed at implementation.

Read on: www.libyadaily.com

MOROCCO

FAST FACTS

- **Total Area:** 446,550 km²
- **Total Population:** 34,343,219
- **Population Growth:** 1.505%
- **Unemployment Rate:** 15%
- **GDP:** $127 billion
- **GDP per capita:** $3,800
- **GDP growth rate:** 2.1%

SETTLEMENTS STRUCTURE

- **Capital City:** Rabat
  1,636,600 pop
  3,917,000 (metro. area)
- **Second City:** Casablanca
  3,397,000 pop
- **Density:** 77 pop/km²
- **Urban Population:** 59%

Political and administrative organisation
Constitutional monarchy composed of 16 regions, 62 departments and 4 municipalities.

Administrative competence for planning
The Ministry of Housing and Planning is in charge of the preparation and coordination of planning legislation. Technical planning agencies are under the aegis of the Ministry; municipalities are weak but are consulted in the process of drawing up strategic development plans (SDAU). Physical development plans (PA) and regulations are produced by public planning agencies under the aegis of the ministry.

Main planning legislation
Planning Act 1992 and Decentralisation Legislation and Administrative Reform 1997. In 1999 a planning law reform was proposed. In 2002 there was an attempt of planning decentralisation but without strengthening the technical competence and finances of local authorities. The 2004 proposal attributes municipalities more repressive planning responsibilities.

Planning and implementation instruments
Strategic planning consists of SDAU: structure plan for urban agglomerations for land use and transportation, investment, infrastructure policies, etc. for a 25 year time horizon. Statutory procedures consist of drawing up the PA, the spatial development and land use plan, and to translate the SDAU into a statutory instrument, valid for a period of ten years, during which no derogations are permitted. At the operational level, regulations control land division and there exist general development control codes.

Development control
Development control is carried out by the municipalities. There exist stringent sanctioning mechanisms against illegal land division and construction, however in the light of urbanisation pressures these measures tend to be difficult to enforce.

Planning system in practice
The planning system with its long term time horizons is criticised for its rigidity, inefficiency and lack of realism, inciting unrealistically high investment into infrastructure. As plans are normalised documents they cannot take into account local specificities, nor do they seem to be able to prevent illegal settlements in urban peripheries. Conversely, lack of land registration is necessary for development but not compulsory and this ambiguity hampers legal development. De facto planning tends to be post hoc and to follow real development. Moreover, economic strategies and programmes are not integrated in physical development.

Read on: www.matee.gov.ma

TUNISIA

FAST FACTS

- **Total Area:** 163,610 km²
- **Total Population:** 10,383,577
- **Population Growth:** 0.989%
- **Unemployment Rate:** 13.9%
- **GDP:** $77.16 billion
- **GDP per capita:** $7,500
- **GDP growth rate:** 6.3%

SETTLEMENTS STRUCTURE

- **Capital City:** Tunis
  - 699,700 pop
  - 1,660,300 (metro. area)
- **Second City:** Sfax
  - 265,131 pop
- **Density:** 63 pop/km²
- **Urban Population:** 64%

Political and administrative organisation
Republic with a presidential regime. It is composed of 24 provinces (governorate), 260 delegations, 2050 communities (imades) and 264 municipalities.

Administrative competence for planning
The nation state, through its ministry of works, housing and spatial planning remains responsible for most planning: national, regional, special protection, operational planning. With decentralisation introduced in 1994 municipalities and/or public operators, such as the housing real estate agency, and the land management agencies of tourism and industry, are competent for local land use plans. Private developers - or whoever intends to build housing estates - have rights to propose land subdivisions.

Main planning legislation
Planning Act 1994 (CATU: code de l'aménagement et de l'urbanisme).

Planning and implementation instruments
There is regulatory and operational planning. The main plans are: SDATN: national spatial plan; SDA: structure plan for built up areas and sensitive areas; departmental plan; PAU: urban land use plan; PAD: detailed plan; land division plan and operational plan for large projects. Any extension of building land is regulated by the planning system.

Development control
Development control is carried out by technical services of large municipalities; the state is responsible for all other areas, in cooperation with operators (e.g. utilities, transportation). Permits for land subdivisions area issued either by the regional or the local authorities.

Planning system in practice
The urban development plans - PAU - tend to be weak. Just over half of them are implemented, while the realisation of planned infrastructure remains below the foreseen level. Infrastructure plans are often devised separately from PAU. PAU are essentially tools for development control and land division, they are not suitable for spatial development strategy. They become obsolete quickly as they are overruled by derogations for developers, state public operators and residents. This situation also favours the generation of illegal settlements, which tend to be integrated post hoc by the state. Often not respected due to derogations the PAU tends not to conform with SDAU, in contradicton with what the law requires. Development on the ground often overtakes also the other structure plans which are hampered by weak vertical integration and tenuous horizontal administrative coordination at state level. Foreign investment obtains preferential treatment, sometimes to the detriment of environmental objetives.

Read on: www.ins.nat.tn; http://admi.net/world/tn; www.host-web.net/atu

ANGOLA

FAST FACTS

- **Total Area:** 1,246,700 km²
- **Total Population:** 12,531,357
- **Population Growth:** 2.136%
- **Unemployment Rate:** 50%
- **GDP:** $80.95 billion
- **GDP per capita:** $6,500
- **GDP growth rate:** 16.3%

SETTLEMENTS STRUCTURE

- **Capital City:** Luanda
  2,297,200 pop
- **Second City:** Huamboca
  171,000 pop
- **Density:** 10 pop/km²
- **Urban Population:** 37%

Political and administrative organisation
Republic composed of 18 provinces and 158 municipalities.

Administrative competence for planning
The National Ministry for Urban Affairs and the Environment is responsible for the national spatial development strategy and housing policy, together with government offices in the provinces which enjoy local autonomy. Luanda has a planning agency which coordinates spatial planning and urban management on behalf of the province. Ad hoc bodies are in charge of implementing urgent planning needs, e.g. housing and infrastructure.

Main planning legislation
First Urbanisation Plan 1942, 1998 Environmental Law, Spatial and Urban Planning Law 2004. The Land Act 2004 regulates land ownership and transaction and property rights of denationalised land. Ordinances are regulating housing allocation and land subdivision.

Planning and implementation instruments
The national level issues a framework for the spatial settlement system and national infrastructure. Spatial, regional and land use planning is undertaken at provincial, regional and municipal levels. Spatial strategic plans were submitted to public debate in 2005 and the General Regulation of Territorial, Urban and Rural Plans was approved in 2006. Their implementation remains unlikely considering the reality of illegal settlements, rapid urbanisation, and damages from the civil war. Municipalities produce global (spatial master plans), sectoral and special municipal plans for urban and rural areas, together with urban management procedures.

Development control
Development control is the task of the municipality, but the pace and intensity of changes due to urbanisation tend to overtake planned development. Ad hoc bodies are carrying out large scale projects for housing and infrastructure instead.

Planning system in practice
The planning system set up in a country recovering from a long civil war will take time to become operational while rapid urbanisation needs to be accommodated with the means available. The majority of provincial governors and municipal administrators are well aware that development of their cities and regions can only be possible through planned interventions. Much effort has been focused on promoting local plans, master plans, detail plans and spatial plans. Better connections between urban and rural planning should assist in containing the migratory flows to cities which lack infrastructure to receive these populations.

Read on: www.angola.org

BOTSWANA ≡

Political and administrative organisation
Republic composed of 8 provinces, 10 rural and 5 urban districts.

Administrative competence for planning
The Ministry of Land and Housing is responsible for planning at national level. The national settlement policy divides the country into 4 planning regions under the department of town and regional planning which determine the spatial distribution of resources. They also devise a regional settlement strategy, master plans and integrated land use plans. Local authorities (tribal administration, land boards, district administration and district and urban councils) are responsible for local physical planning.

Main planning legislation
Local Government (District Council) Act 1865, Township Act 1999, Town and Country Planning Act 1977, Development Control Code 1995, and Urban Development Standards, 1992 applied in existing settlements and as a guide for new ones.

Planning and implementation instruments
There is a long term vision for 2016. A National physical development plan is also foreseen. The Town and Country Planning Board is coordinating the planning input of various ministries. Legislation is defining 17 urban planning areas where urban standards apply. Economic strategies are laid down in the national development plan, district development plans and urban development plans. Physical development plans contain a written statement and maps. Regional master plans seek to redress regional disparity, while integrated district and urban land use plans aim to protect people and property from natural hazards, to conserve natural resources and address economic, social, environmental, physical and spatial management issues. Local plans regulate competing interests and incorporate Agenda 21 projects of sustainable development. There is also a systematic monitoring review of all local plans. Implementation programmes, including budgets and designated agencies and environmental impact procedures, have been devised for urban areas and may be introduced in rural areas as well.

FAST FACTS

- **Total Area:** 600,370 km²
- **Total Population:** 1,842,323
- **Population Growth:** 1.434%
- **Unemployment Rate:** 23.8%
- **GDP:** $24.14 billion
- **GDP per capita:** $14,700
- **GDP growth rate:** 4.7%

Development control
Development control consists of issuing permits for physical development and controlling the building process, checking compliance with plans, imposing restrictions and facilitating legal land acquisition.

SETTLEMENTS STRUCTURE

- **Capital City:** Gaborone
  195,000 pop
- **Second City:** Francistown
  113,315 pop
- **Density:** 3 pop/km²
- **Urban Population:** 53%

Planning system in practice
National planning strategy is to stem unsustainable population flows to cities and urban areas by revitalising settlements and their economies in the countryside, as opposed to past investment concentration in urban areas also during colonial times. There is a trend away from foreign planning influences to more indigenous approaches to spatial development. Decentralisation is progressing and will require adjustments to the Town and Country Planning Act, such as the provision of three planning levels. There is growing contradiction between imported, and increasingly challenged planning models and the revival of traditional settlement patterns. The plea is for interdisciplinary and environment friendly planning.

Read on: www.landsandhousing.gov.bw ; www.gov.bw; www.ub.bw

GHANA

FAST FACTS

- **Total Area:** 238,539 km^2
- **Total Population:** 23,382,848
- **Population Growth:** 1.928%
- **Unemployment Rate:** 11%
- **GDP:** $31.23 billion
- **GDP per capita:** $1,400
- **GDP growth rate:** 6.2%

SETTLEMENTS STRUCTURE

- **Capital City:** Accra
  1,661,400 pop
  2,825,800 (metro. area)
- **Second City:** Kumasi
  645,100 pop
- **Density:** 98 pop/km^2
- **Urban Population:** 46%

Political and administrative organisation
Republic composed of 10 regions, 110 districts, 58 town councils, 622 area councils and 16,000 unit committees.

Administrative competence for planning
Land use and environmental planning is carried out by government departments for the whole country since 1945. The Local and Rural Government Ministry is responsible for the decentralisation of planning, turning 138 District Assemblies into planning authorities. The National Development Planning Commission issues national development strategies for district assemblies and approves all plans. Metropolitan, Municipal and District Assemblies produce development and structure plans and sub districts produce local action plans.

Main planning legislation
The Town and Country Ordinance establishes the government department responsible for spatial planning. PNDC law 207 sets up regional coordination councils formalised in the National Development Planning (Systems) Act 1994. Public Administration Reform legislation 1992-94, includes the Local Government Act and Civil Service Law, seeking to decentralise planning powers and increase public participation.

Planning and implementation instruments
Standards for different categories of settlements are set at national level by the Town and Country Planning Department, which also initiates settlement legislation and monitors its effects. Policies for managing the environment and land resources are incorporated in structure and development plans at district level. Plans are frequently updated to take account of bottom up choices. There are shared GIS facilities.

Development control
District authorities approve planning applications and legal sanctions ensure conformity to plans.

Planning system in practice
Sectoral coordination is lacking due to historic administrative legacy. This leads to conflicts during plan making between various agencies. The same applies to land management which is attributed to over 22 agencies. The Land Administration Project of 2003 aims to remedy at land use plan implementation and transparent land allocation and management. A decentralised system with one stop shops should bring the system closer to land owners and other interested parties in development. The proposed system is expected to be self-financing through levies and charges. However lack of professional staff is inhibiting progress. It also accounts for the lack of completed decentralised plans. Planning education remains too limited and needs expansion, together with technical know how and equipment for planning. While institutional change is progressing, public participation remains poor as traditional exchanges are dominated by small groups.

Read on: www.angola.org

Political and administrative organisation
Republic composed of 7 provinces, 73 districts, divisions and localities and the extra-provincial region of Nairobi and its environs.

Administrative competence for planning
Central government is responsible de facto for all planning. It is devising spatial planning policies for the whole country and preparing regional and local plans. Government departments are constantly changing 'to deal better with stakeholders'. There are no local plans, thus local authorities have difficulties of enforcing development control. The planning profession has a powerful influence on planning.

Main planning legislation
Central government is responsible de facto for all planning. It is devising spatial planning policies for the whole country and preparing regional and local plans. Government departments are constantly changing 'to deal better with stakeholders'. There are no local plans, thus local authorities have difficulties of enforcing development control.

Planning and implementation instruments
There exists a national land use master plan for the whole country. The physical planning handbook is regularly updated. All plans - regional physical development plans, local physical development plans, action plans for market districts, special cross boundary plans - are produced by central government.

Development control
Development control has been put into the hands of local authorities including for unplanned settlements. There is no real public participation.

Planning system in practice
Informal settlements which make up a large part of urbanisation are unsuccessfully controlled by government agents and local authorities. Planning permissions according to local plans, often not available, are subject to local authority service provision. Only two of 68 development plans and one local plan exist despite statutory legislation. Centralisation and restrictive professional practices for planning lead to under-capacity in local administrations. Privatisation of utilities has been introduced in 2005 but only few have been liberated and remain seriously undercapitalised. Other market driven development finds its way mainly into real estate as the country is considered sufficiently stable. However, it takes place without planning as planning procedures remain slow, cumbersome and politicised. Continuous informal housing settlement is also progressing outside planning. Public participation in the planning process remains poor and citizens are unaware of their rights and efforts of awareness raising are undertaken.

FAST FACTS

- **Total Area:** 582,650 km²
- **Total Population:** 37,953,838
- **Population Growth:** 2.758%
- **Unemployment Rate:** 40%
- **GDP:** $57.65 billion
- **GDP per capita:** $1,600
- **GDP growth rate:** 6.3%

SETTLEMENTS STRUCTURE

- **Capital City:** Nairobi
    2,411,900 pop
    3,064,800 (metro. area)
- **Second City:** Mombassa
    712,600 pop
- **Density:** 65 pop/km²
- **Urban Population:** 42%

Read on: www.kenyaweb.com; www.uonbi.ac.ke

FAST FACTS

- **Total Area:** 30,355 km²
- **Total Population:** 2,128,180
- **Population Growth:** 0.129%
- **Unemployment Rate:** 45%
- **GDP:** $3.088 billion
- **GDP per capita:** $1,500
- **GDP growth rate:** 4.8%

SETTLEMENTS STRUCTURE

- **Capital City:** Maseru
  173,700 pop
- **Second City:** Teyateyaneng
  48,869 pop
- **Density:** 70 pop/km²
- **Urban Population:** 18%

Political and administrative organisation
Constitutional monarchy composed of 10 districts, 60 constituencies and 1,093 enumeration areas.

Administrative competence for planning
Under colonial rule, the planning system was ruled by chiefs within districts, abolished after independence. Now the Ministry of local government is in overall control through new district administrators. In 1996, local authorities obtained competences over planning, land management and development control, as well as control over natural resources, environmental protection and land allocation. The districts regulate leases which need to be registered. The municipal councils are responsible for their applications with increased participation. Decentralisation is formalised into District, Ward and Village Development Committees.

Main planning legislation
Town and Country Planning Act 1980/1984, Local Government Act 1996/1997, Agricultural Policy and Capacity Building Project. The Land Management and Administration Act 1999 sets up a land use record (without registration powers though). The Land Bill 2004 replaces the Land Act 1979 to allocate land and formalise the land market.

Planning and implementation instruments
The five year national development plan designates growth centres at three levels of importance, with 4, 11 and 36 centres respectively to ensure even spatial distribution and curb rural exodus. At district level planning deals with resource allocation, local development and coordination, as well as plan approval, but de facto this remains under government control. Ward chiefs can submit development projects proposed at village level to districts.

Development control
Theoretically it is the responsibility of the lowest tier but in reality the districts control it and through them central government. The lowest tier can propose own projects for higher tier approval.

Planning system in practice
Despite clear regulation of land attribution and control, illegal land subdivision and settlements are widespread and take place even in specifically designated selected development areas and bypass the three tier planning system. Nevertheless, initiatives of district development coordinating committees have led projects to remedy some of these issues. Similarly to informal housing production, unregulated trading is occurring throughout existing settlements as part of the informal economy which is driving the large amount of poor population and contravene basic planning principles of hygiene and existing legislation. As a result, urban life is congested and insalubrious despite planning principles and international aid programmes.

Read on: www.lesotho.gov.ls; www.nul.ls

MALAWI

FAST FACTS

- **Total Area:** 118.484 km²
- **Total Population:** 13,931,831
- **Population Growth:** 2.39 %
- **Unemployment Rate:** -
- **GDP:** $10.47 billion
- **GDP per capita:** $800
- **GDP growth rate:** 5.7%

SETTLEMENTS STRUCTURE

- **Capital City:** Lilongwe
  499,200 pop
- **Second City:** Blantyre
  547,500 pop
- **Density:** 118 pop/km²
- **Urban Population:** 17%

Political and administrative organisation
People's Democratic Republic. Presidential regime. The Republic is composed of 9 regions, 48 provinces (wilaya), 553 districts (diara) and 1541 municipalities.

Administrative competence for planning
The state is responsible for the national and the regional plans; the wilaya are competent for the provincial plans and inter-communal arrangements. The municipalities are competent for drawing up their own plans, including detail plans.

Main planning legislation
In the absence of a formal planning act (under preparation), a number of complementary regulations determine national, regional and local plan making and implementation. They are the Framework Legislation for National Spatial Planning 1987, and Land Use Planning Regulations 1990.

Planning and implementation instruments
The planning system is hierarchical with requirement of vertical compatibility between plans.
SNAT: national spatial plan
SRAT: regional spatial plan grouping some 9 wilayas
PAW: structure plan for wilayas
PDAU: municipal or inter-municipal structure and development plan, compulsory for all 1541 communes
POS: municipal land use plan, required to be compatible with PDAU, determining COS, CES, formal design and building rules, prepared by professionals
Land subdivision can be initiated by developers.

Development control
Land subdivision, building and demolition permits are the responsibility of the municipalities.

Planning system in practice
There is a lack of compatibility between different levels of planning despite legal requirements. This is partly due to an uneven data base and lack of coordinating procedures. Other deficiencies include lack of consultation and insufficient technical competence of decision makers and administrators. Weak instruments of implementation and the lengthy process of plan making and approval require frequent plan revision. This is not helped by political pressures to abolish democratic governance structures at the loal level which are needed to support bottom up initiatives and obtain a share of scarce resources for infrastructure provision.

Read on: www.mhu.gov.dz; http://63.70.212.91/
www.algeria-market.com; www.univ-constantine-dz; www.ceneap.com.dz

NAMIBIA

FAST FACTS

- **Total Area:** 2,825,418 km²
- **Total Population:** 2,088,669
- **Population Growth:** 0.947%
- **Unemployment Rate:** 5.3%
- **GDP:** $10.67 billion
- **GDP per capita:** $5,200
- **GDP growth rate:** 4.5%

SETTLEMENTS STRUCTURE

- **Capital City:** Windhoek
  233,529 pop.
  Summer capital:
  Swakopmund, 26,200 pop
- **Second City:** Rundu
  44,413 pop
- **Density:** 0,79 pop/km²
- **Urban Population:** 34%

Political and administrative organisation
Republic composed of 13 administrative regions.

Administrative competence for planning
The National Planning Commission is devising national development strategies and resource allocation through a five year plan. Regional and local councils are responsible for physical planning. Regional Development Coordinating Committees are seeing to the effectiveness and coordination of planning. Regions and local authorities have considerable autonomy, including tax raising powers.

Main planning legislation
The Town Planning Ordinance 1954 and Township and Division Ordinance 1963 are regulating spatial development with regard to efficiency and welfare. They will be consolidated into a single Act and include environmental matters. The Regional Councils Act and Local Authorities Act 1992 allocate planning competences of these bodies, regulate physical development processes and building regulation.

Planning and implementation instruments
Land use plans drawn up only by local authorities until now include land title information whose rights are restricted in the absence of a plan. Larger cities also issue non statutory guidelines regarding conservation and environmental matters. Local authorities are also in charge of settlement administration, including budgeting and financing of communal infrastructure and the attribution of added land value.

Development control
Land use changes are usually initiated by private owners. Local authorities are in charge of development control but higher levels have final approval rights. Tribal land rights are regulated differently in the north.

Planning system in practice
Devolution and realistic notification of development is ineffective in the existing planning system. Thus alternative solutions have to be sought through direct information exchange on specific sites and negotiation processes among interested parties. This would have the benefit of resolving local conflicts outside cumbersome judicial procedures. Dual legislation has led to power duplication at the centre where both the Namibia Planning Advisory Board and the Townships Board have conflicting advisory status, thus streamlining has become necessary. This is especially needed in the light of the lack of qualified human resources to fulfil all the newly introduced compulsory planning functions. Most crucially the integration of environmental matters into planning is lacking which enables rigid zoning to prevail in reality despite the political will to incorporate sustainability principles into the planning system.

Read on: www.op.gov.na; www.oag.gov.na; www.unam.na

FAST FACTS

- **Total Area:** 923,768 km²
- **Total Population:** 138,283,240
- **Population Growth:** 2.382%
- **Unemployment Rate:** 5.8%
- **GDP:** $294.8 billion
- **GDP per capita:** $2,200
- **GDP growth rate:** 6,5%

SETTLEMENTS STRUCTURE

- **Capital City:** Abuja
  165,700 pop
  590,400 (metro. area)
- **Largest City:** Lagos
  5,686,000 pop
  11,135,000 (metro. area)
- **Density:** 148 pop/km²
- **Urban Population:** 48%

Political and administrative organisation
Federal Republic composed of 36 regions, 1 federal capital territory and 774 local councils.

Administrative competence for planning
The Commissioner for Land, Surveys and Country Planning, selects planning consultants who prepare plans, sometimes with the urban development board which is responsible for implementation. The Ministry of Works, Housing and Urban Development allocates land, and the Urban Planning Board issues development permits.

Main planning legislation
Town Improvement Ordinance 1863, Land Proclamation Law 1946, Nigerian Town and Country Planning Ordinance based on the British Town and Country Planning Act 1923, Land Use Act, as well as a national urban development policy guidance. The laws on regional governments and regions have been changing four regions into a proliferation of states. The 1992 legislation has partially replaced colonial based planning law.

Planning and implementation instruments
The planning system is very centralised. The federal government has planning departments at local levels to divide and allocate land for development for housing on federal land. Regional development plans regulate economic, social and environmental development. Urban development plans are drawn up by state governments aimed at the local urbanisation process without the involvement of local government or executive mayors, except in Lagos.

Development control
Development control as well as approval of plans is in the hands of the Urban Development Board at national level which is carrying out site inspections itself to verify conformity to plans and permits.

Planning system in practice
Planning has a long history since colonial times and is totally embedded in bureaucratic structures in the hands of the civil service. This makes the planning process complex and slow, notwithstanding corruption and lack of skilled personnel. Despite stringent planning controls a lot of informal development takes place. In response, informal development permits are issued, especially on urban fringes. Planning remains very bureaucratic and complex and lacks human resources, thus it is not able to adjust to fast changing circumstances and especially to rapid urban growth due to rural urban migration and regional migratory movements. Often developers proceed without permission, due to undue delays of the planning process. Decentralisation legislation is expected to remedy some of the bureaucratic hurdles of the planning process, especially at the local level of implementation.

Read on: www.lagosstate.gov.ng; www.unima.mw
www.unam.na; www.ui.edu.ng; www.environmentnigeria.org

FAST FACTS

- **Total Area:** 1,219,912 km²
- **Total Population:** 43,786,115
- **Population Growth:** -0.501%
- **Unemployment Rate:** 24.2%
- **GDP:** $467.6 billion
- **GDP per capita:** $10,600
- **GDP growth rate:** 5%

SETTLEMENTS STRUCTURE

- **Capital Cities:** Pretoria (leg)
  1,249,700 pop,
  Bloemfontein (jur)
  378,000 pop.
  Cape Town (adm)
  2,733,000 pop
  3,140,600 (metro. area)
- **Density:** 36 pop/km²
- **Urban Population:** 58%

Political and administrative organisation
Republic composed of 9 provinces, 47 districts and 245 municipalities and 3 capitals (administrative, legislative, judicial)

Administrative competence for planning
Municipalities are the drivers of socio-economic and spatial development and planning delivery.

Main planning legislation
Development Facilitating Act 1995, Municipal Systems Act 2000 (municipal structure and demarcation acts 1998), National Spatial Development Perspective 2006-2014. Great emphasis is laid on the environment in urban and regional development: in the Constitution (environmental clause 24); National Environmental Management Act 1998; many sectoral acts, etc. The Town and Regional Planners Act 1984, replaced by the planning professions bill will give a definition of planning. Land reform and restitution is key to planning and dealt with in various acts.

Planning and implementation instruments
Planning aims at integrated, compact, liveable settlements without sprawl and applies to both formal and informal settlements. Urban strategies and 5 year statutory integrated development plans (IDP) are implementation instruments which guide all municipal spatial priorities, management and decision making. Planned integration includes a spatial framework, financial plan, sectoral programme and projects and land reform. The department of provincial and local government is responsible for implementing IDPs, while the department of land affairs regulates the planning profession. Projects are implemented by service providers with local authorities. At regional level development commissions advise the provinces.

Development control
Development control is administered by land use and environmental management systems which includes public participation. Town planning schemes exist in certain parts (defined in previous provincial town planning ordinances).

Planning system in practice
A new sophisticated planning system was set up after the profound changes in 1994 with the aim to create uniformity in all areas and to provide greater equity throughout the country. Implementing these changes took time and evaluation may be premature. However, a clear focus is on service delivery and should facilitate implementation which is possibly hampered by lack of human resources and institutional capacity. Meanwhile there remains a strong division between formal planning and informal development. Moreover, an environmental enforcement agency is lacking to monitor and implement the pledged sustainability principles.

Read on: http://land.pwv.gov.za; www.ppdiv.mil.za; www.puk.ac.za; www.arp.uct. ac.za; www.dit.ac.za; www.ukzn.ac.za/arch/planning/planning.htm; www.saplanners. org.za; www.wits.ac.za/planning; www.univen.ac.za

FAST FACTS

- **Total Area:** 2,505,810 km²
- **Total Population:** 40,218,455
- **Population Growth:** 2.134%
- **Unemployment Rate:** 18.7%
- **GDP:** 107.8 billion $
- **GDP per capita:** $2,500
- **GDP growth rate:** 12.8 %

SETTLEMENTS STRUCTURE

- **Capital City:** Khartoum
  1,397,900 pop
  5,717,300 (metro. area)
- **Second City:** Ordurman
  2,103,900 pop
- **Density:** 16 pop/km²
- **Urban Population:** 41%

Political and administrative organisation
Federal republic composed of 26 states (wilayat), municipalities (mahaliyat), localities and popular committees.

Administrative competence for planning
The national level devises national spatial strategies and approves state structure plans. The state level is in charge of plan making and development control of land use under central ministerial guidance, and it approves lower tier plans and housing programmes. Regions (states) are responsible for development and land use plans and can devise their own planning legislation, which is not done in practice. The municipalities are in charge of maintaining infrastructure and landscapes and make inputs to village plans, but ratification of all planning stays with the central government.

Main planning legislation
The Physical Planning and Land Disposal Act 1994, replacing the various Town Re-Planning Acts from colonial times constitute the framework legislation of spatial planning at federal level requiring licenses for all physical development. The Local Government Act 2003 is specifying the planning powers of lower tier authorities including over own bye laws and building codes. Several acts regulate settlement rights through land registration and surveying. There exists an Environmental Conservation Act 1975.

Planning and implementation instruments
Overall planning is carried out at the national level by the federal administration which steers lower tier development. However, the states and the municipalities are responsible for devising and enforcing the development plans of their own areas, including environmental protection and preservation of historic heritage, as well as change of use. They are also in charge of containing or eliminating squatter settlements

Development control
The state and municipal levels are responsible for controlling development and land use within their statutory remits according to their plans.

Planning system in practice
In reality land use plans are only prepared by cities, mainly the capital, and no regional plans have been devised. Lack of qualified manpower and adverse socio-political conditions account for the inefficient use of planning powers at regional and state levels. Informal settlement is widespread and creates sprawl on city fringes, uncontrollable by formal planning measures. Oil wealth is expected to improve this.

Read on: www.sudan.net

SWAZILAND

FAST FACTS

- **Total Area:** 17,363 km²
- **Total Population:** 1,128,814
- **Population Growth:** -0.41%
- **Unemployment Rate:** 40%
- **GDP:** $5.424 billion
- **GDP per capita:** $4,800
- **GDP growth rate:** 1.6%

SETTLEMENTS STRUCTURE

- **Capital City:** Mbabane
  69,000 pop;
  royal and legislative capital:
  Lobamba, circa 5,000

- **Second City:** Manzini
  75,000 pop

- **Density:** 65 pop/km²

- **Urban Population:** 24%

Political and administrative organisation
Constitutional monarchy composed of combination of western and tribal structure, composed of 4 districts and 55 local authorities (tribal chiefdoms).

Administrative competence for planning
There are different administrative structures for urban and rural areas where the tribal system prevails. The Ministry for Housing and Urban Development is responsible for national spatial policies. Cities and towns are in charge of physical planning, bye laws, local taxation and development control.

Main planning legislation
The Urban Government Act 1969 is the main legislation, last amended in 2003. Legislationa includes the Land Utilisation Act 1951, Building Act 1968, Town Planning Act 1961, Human Settlement Act 1988 amended 1992, Rating Act 1967 amended in 1997, and the Peri-urban Management Policy of 1997.

Planning and implementation instruments
The system is centralised with the King holding most powers. The national physical development plan (NPDP) is elaborated by the Ministry which is responsible for national planning policies. But on the whole, regional and local planning are done ad hoc according to perceived needs. There are no formal local planning authorities and regional sectoral planning is undertaken by the centre which is also responsible for resource allocation. Cities are producing town planning schemes consisting of structure plans (20-25 years), development plans and development codes.

Development control
In cities development control is carried out by the local authority which has surveying and enforcement capacity. In the rural areas tribal customs rule development.

Planning system in practice
There is little relation between the existing planning system and reality. Way over half the population lives in fast growing informal settlements. They seem difficult to control or upgrade outside the city jurisdiction despite international assistance, as responsibilities remain unclear. The scale of basic infrastructure needs and the health hazards are way beyond the material and technical means of either central or local governments. The current planning system and resources are not able to supply even the most basic requirements of utilities, such as water, sewage energy supply. A paraphernalia of new policies has been devised but implementation seems doubtful. As the country is essential rural where tribal customs prevail it is foreseen to train chiefs in planning, in the hope that this would improve the situation.

Read on: http://home.swazi.com
www.gov.sz

FAST FACTS

- **Total Area:** 17,363 km²
- **Total Population:** 1,128,814
- **Population Growth:** -0.41%
- **Unemployment Rate:** 40%
- **GDP:** $5.424 billion
- **GDP per capita:** $4,800
- **GDP growth rate:** 1,6%

SETTLEMENTS STRUCTURE

- **Capital City:** Dodoma
  164,500 pop
- **Largest City:** Dar es Salaam
  2,489,800 pop
- **Density:** 65 pop/km²
- **Urban Population:** 38%

Political and administrative organisation

Republic composed of 26 regions, 117 districts (92 rural and 25 urban). Urban and rural districts are further subdivided into wards and sub-wards or villages respectively.

Administrative competence for planning

The national government is responsible for national 5 year plans and budgets and regional plans. Rural districts are producing local physical plans; urban districts draw up master plans, annual programmes, urban development and land use plans.

Main planning legislation

The Town and Country Planning Act 1956 was revised after independence. It is the main planning legislation under review to deal with illegal settlements. The Land Ordinance 1923 regulates land tenure. It became the Land and Village Act in 1999. There are also Local Government, Forest, Wildlife and Survey Ordinances. Other spatial policies are sectoral: human settlements, transportation, environment, together with guidelines. Aiming for rural development after independence, the country adopted socialism and self reliance and land was nationalised in 1962 when compulsory purchase powers were set up. The 1995 Land Policy introduced compensation. Recent change took place from technocratic to participatory planning.

Planning and implementation instruments

Plan preparation and approval is decentralised while professional planning education rests with the government. Rural plans are produced by the rural district authorities. More flexible strategic planning and environmental planning and management is done by all districts (bottom up).

Development control

It is regulated to some extent and implemented by the districts and for normative plans by the villages.

Planning system in practice

Change from a socialist to a mixed economy had planning implications which are being dealt with by increasing participation of the private sector but not civil society which develops alternative approaches to land use with greater active participation. Plans exist for most areas but are not followed, especially in rural areas. Urbanisation continues to produce unmanageable illegal settlements (70% in urban areas) while developers handle formal development, despite the state owning the land but moving towards formal property rights. Planning remains dominated be experts and the centre, although civic society based approaches are emerging which may be more able to deal with development in a poor country.

Read on: www.udsm.ac.tz

ZAMBIA

FAST FACTS

- **Total Area:** 754,614 km²
- **Total Population:** 11,669,534
- **Population Growth:** 1.654%
- **Unemployment Rate:** 50%
- **GDP:** $15.93 billion
- **GDP per capita:** $1,400
- **GDP growth rate:** 6%

SETTLEMENTS STRUCTURE

- **Capital City:** Lusaka
  1,265,000 pop
  1,773,300 (metro. area)
- **Second City:** Ndola
  349,300 pop
- **Density:** 15 pop/km²
- **Urban Population:** 37%

Political and administrative organisation
Republic composed of 9 provinces and 73 districts.

Administrative competence for planning
Since independence in 1964, the Central government is in charge of planning at all levels. The Ministry of Local Government and Housing MLGH is responsible for national planning but, conflictingly, the Ministry of Finance is entrusted with national economic planning, budgeting and regional planning, together with the provincial administration in the hands of state representatives. City, municipal and district councils draw up local plans but districts are not planning authorities and rural planning is done by the state. The minister appoints planning authorities and directs the planning process.

Main planning legislation
The Town Planning Ordinance 1929 was to establish town planning schemes and planning boards. After independence, it became the Town and Country Planning Act 1964, amended in 1997. Other legislation includes the Housing (Statutory and Improvement Areas) Act 1974, the Land Acquisition Act, Rating Act, Local Government Act, Public Health Act, Environmental Protection and Pollution Control Act, Land and Deeds Registry Act, Survey Act, Housing Act, National Heritage Conservation Act and Tourism Act.

Planning and implementation instruments
Land use is based on a zoning system. Spatial plans are subordinate to economic planning and lack institutional resources to make effective provision for future generations. There are regional plans, structure plans replacing development plans (1997) showing statutory housing areas, local detail and layout plans (housing and improvement areas).

Development control
Development control is carried out by city and local authorities, which need government permits to draw up their own public development or rezoning plans. Use classes exist for permitted development.

Planning system in practice
Planning system and procedures are too centralised, detailed and prescriptive to suit the realities of the country, including illegal settlements which seem to have become uncontrollable. Lack of public participation leads to non compliance while decentralisation is not implemented. Lack of overall spatial planning strategy lost in myriad of procedures and decentralisation would not work without local capacity building. Greater participation of the private sector is sought. Planners are blamed for squatter settlements and environmental degradation as they are perceived unable to adapt to new socio-economic conditions.

Read on: www.cbu.edu.zm

ZIMBABWE

FAST FACTS

- **Total Area:** 390,580 km²
- **Total Population:** 12,382,920
- **Population Growth:** 0.568%
- **Unemployment Rate:** 80%
- **GDP:** $6.186 billion
- **GDP per capita:** $500
- **GDP growth rate:** -6%

SETTLEMENTS STRUCTURE

- **Capital City:** Harare
  1,919,700 pop
  2,331,400 (metro. area)
- **Second City:** Bulawayo
  965,000 pop
- **Density:** 33 pop/km²
- **Urban Population:** 36%

Political and administrative organisation

Republic composed of 8 provinces and 27 rural and 24 urban councils, divided into wards and villages.

Administrative competence for planning

The presidency has ultimate powers over planning decisions. It can set up and dismantle statutory regional councils and reverse lower tier decisions. Provincial authorities are not elected, can be created at any time by the president. They operate without their own budget and oversee rural wards. Non elected lowest tier competences are very low.

Main planning legislation

The Town and Country Planning Act 1933 replaced in 1945, 1976, 1996, inherited from colonial times, required amendments to reflect local conditions. The Region, Town and Country Planning Act 1996 vests planning powers, land subdivision and acquisition, development control in urban councils and rural districts. Other relevant legislation encompasses Urban Councils Act 1996. Rural District Council Act 1988. Provincial Councils and Administration Act 1985. The Land Act, Deeds Registry Act, Local Government Act and various acts on utilities and the environment are also relevant to planning.

Planning and implementation instruments

The state prepares annual economic development plans. Local authorities have vested powers to draw up master plans with economic development goals, local development, subject and priority plans including conservation, as well as land use control accordingly under ministerial direction. Ad hoc regional planning councils draw up regional strategies and oversee or carry out planning de facto in rural and urban councils where they have delegated ministerial powers. Local plans include a statement and land use zoning maps, suited to the control ideology. Documents include a development local subject and local priority plan.

Development control

Local authorities are in charge of development control and enforcement involving negotiation, except for state projects and development with special consent. They often lack qualified staff. Measures are in place for bottom up participation.

Planning system in practice

The colonial planning acts with weak links with economic planning do not reflect current communal living needs in urban areas. Political interference weakens the planning profession and rigidity of development control cannot cope with rapid urbanisation and prevents innovative initiatives (e.g. operation refuse disposal in poor areas). Local authorities continue to provide housing without services but with de facto agriculture. Land for low income housing is traded in the private market or allocated by local authorities.

Read on: www.zimfa.gov.zw; http://uzweb.uz.ac.zw/social/rup

America

NORTH AMERICA
Canada
Mexico
USA

CENTRAL AMERICA
Barbados
Costa Rica
El Salvador
Guatemala
Honduras
Trinidad and Tobago

SOUTH AMERICA
Argentina
Bolivia
Brazil
Chile
Colombia
Guyana
Paraguay
Peru
Uruguay
Venezuela

CANADA

FAST FACTS

- **Total Area:** 9,984,670 km²
- **Total Population:** 33,212,696
- **Population Growth:** 0.83%
- **Unemployment Rate:** 5.9%
- **GDP:** $1.274 trillion
- **GDP per capita:** $38,200
- **GDP growth rate:** 2.7%

SETTLEMENTS STRUCTURE

- **Capital City:** Ottawa
    1,142,700 pop
- **Largest City:** Toronto
    5,203,600 pop
- **Density:** 3 pop/km²
- **Urban Population:** 81%

Political and administrative organisation

Constitutional monarchy with a parliamentary democracy, confederation composed of 10 provinces, 3 territories and 1,640 municipalities.

Administrative competence for planning

The national government aims for 'peace order and good government', and is planning for installations of national interest and housing policies. The provinces are upper tier local government with great autonomy. They are in charge of land titling and management as well as urban and rural planning and law making. Counties and groups of municipalities exist in urban centred metropolitan regions and in resource regions. Local municipalities are responsible for detailed plans and development control but have no constitutional rights.

Main planning legislation

Provinces have law making powers in the field of planning. Municipal acts are devised by provinces. Planning acts define plan making procedures for regions and municipalities. Environmental Protection Acts, Historic Preservation Acts, Protection of Agricultural Land Act (Quebec). Provincial policy guidance also influences planning.

Planning and implementation instruments

In an administrative rather than discretionary planning system, regional or metropolitan plans are general spatial planning frameworks designating broad land uses and transportation, as the basis for general plans, strategic plans, master plans, official land use plans, detail plans, neighbourhood plans, etc. revised every five years. There are also building regulations drawn up by the municipalities. Local authorities produce pro-active implementation programmes with public investment and incentives for private sector development, especially for brown field site regeneration. There is good vertical cooperation for special site regeneration, economic aims or social spatial cohesion. Large projects are implemented through consensus based public private partnerships. Public participation is widespread.

Development control

Local authorities are responsible for development control according to a zoning law and other land use controls devised by them. It is automatic if the proposal is conform to the local plan.

Planning system in practice

With rapid urbanisation and urban sprawl, planning in urban areas at municipal level hampered coherent development. Thus the states and provinces imposed an amalgamation of municipalities into metropolitan urban regions despite public opposition to carry out comprehensive integrated development strategies. As municipalities finances are stretched fiscal reform is needed for satisfactory spatial development.

Read on: www.icurr.org; www.ouq.qc.ca; www.amo.on.ca; www.omb.gov.on.ca;
www.inrs-ucs.uquebec.ca; www.aacip.com; www.aarq.qc.ca; www.0uq.qc.ca;

MEXICO

FAST FACTS

- **Total Area:** 1,972,550 km²
- **Total Population:** 109,955,400
- **Population Growth:** 1.142%
- **Unemployment Rate:** 3.7%
- **GDP:** $1.353 trillion
- **GDP per capita:** $12,500
- **GDP growth rate:** 3%

SETTLEMENTS STRUCTURE

- **Capital City:** Mexico City
  8,591,309 pop
  19,013,000 (metro. area)

- **Second City:** Guadalajara
  1,665,800 pop

- **Density:** 56 pop/km²

- **Urban Population:** 76%

Political and administrative organisation
Federal republic composed of 31 states, 9 regions, 2,645 municipalities and a Federal District composed of 16 delegations.

Administrative competence for planning
Three levels of government - federal, state and municipal - share planning responsibilities. The federal government is responsible for devising a National Development Plan while the states draw up urban development programmes and are responsible for primary allocation of land use. The municipalities elaborate more detailed zoning and urban development plans and are in charge of approving and managing them. The Secretariat of Social Development has powers over spatial organisation, urban and regional development and the provision of land reserves.

Main planning legislation
Article 26 of the political Constitution lays down conditions for the planning system. Relevant legislation is Planning Law, General Law for Human Settlements, Federal Pact and Organic Law of the Federal Public Administration.

Planning and implementation instruments
The National Development Plan 2001-2006 provides, inter alia, the framework for urban planning. It is the main policy instrument to regulate Mexico's development, encompassing human and social development, quality of growth, sustainability and territorial integrity. The Secretariat of Social Development produces the national programme for urban development and spatial organisation under its remit for spatial and regional development. It also constitutes public land banks. Federal legislation defines planning rights and obligations of the states, subjected to general state development strategies. They define urban land uses and land to be urbanised. Municipalities draw up, approve and implement their own detailed land use plans. They can also draw up regional development plans in conformity with state plans and programmes. Urban centres (expansion or creation of new ones) form separate levels of planning and are the main tool of regulating the urbanisation process.

Development control
Municipalities are responsible for development control of their own plans which they also approve. They also issue building permits.

Planning system in practice
Planning is considered too centralised and unable to accommodate the great diversity of Mexico, its territory, people and cultures. It also is not sufficiently differentiated at local level. Municipal needs are not accommodated in the broad national policies and programmes. Conversely planning provides equity.

Read on: www.semarnat.gob.mx; www.fcarm.org.mx; www.rniu.buap.mx;
www.planeacion.unam.mx; www.amau.org.mx; www.camsam.org; Www.arq.unam.mx

FAST FACTS

- **Total Area:** 9,826,630 km²
- **Total Population:** 303,824,646
- **Population Growth:** 0.883%
- **Unemployment Rate:** 4.6%
- **GDP:** $13.86 trillion
- **GDP per capita:** $ 46,000
- **GDP growth rate:** 2.2%

SETTLEMENTS STRUCTURE

- **Capital City:** Washington
  570,898 pop
- **Largest City:** New York
  8,085,742 pop
  18,498,000 (metro area)
- **Density:** 31 pop/km²
- **Urban Population:** 81%

Political and administrative organisation

Federal republic composed of 50 states, 1 Federal District, counties and municipalities.

Administrative competence for planning

The federal government has limited planning powers. Institutions involved are the federal government, Department of Housing and Urban Development; state administrations for own laws and responsible for implementing sectoral federal laws (e.g. environmental impact statements), counties, cities, municipalities, and coalitions between these levels. New urbanism was initiated by the planning profession to achieve better urban conditions countrywide, by means of liveable communities and compact cities near transportation nodes.

Main planning legislation

Federal property is regulated by federal legislation. Federal legislation determines what physical changes are subjected to planning, implemented by the states or regional and local agencies: e.g. National Environmental Policy Act, Clean Water Act, Clean Air Act, Resource Recovery and Conservation Act, Inter-modal Surface Transportation Efficiency Act, Federal Housing programmes. State legislation encompasses growth management programmes and vertical planning coordination.

Planning and implementation instruments

States implement their own laws (vertical coordination of planning, growth management programmes). Subsidiarity which underpins planning legislation and practice means that most planning powers rest with lower tier authorities or sectoral agencies. Counties and cities produce spatial development strategies, community, land use and zoning plans, land subdivision laws and building codes. These instruments are often linked to infrastructure investment plans.

Development control

At federal level, certain types of land use emissions are controlled. At county and municipality level, the federal level controls conformity to laws and municipalities conformity to building codes.

Planning system in practice

The USA planning system is subjected to strong property and land use rights which may clash with public concern for environmental protection and resource management. Development is mainly initiated and conducted by the private sector and legislation is meant to support these initiatives not hamper them. There is a great diversity of planning philosophies and practices at state and local levels.

Read on: www.nps.gov; www.fs.fed.us; www.dod.gov; www.blm.gov;
www.epa.gov/compliance/nepa; www.epa.gov; www.epa.gov; www.istea.org;
www.planning.org

FAST FACTS

- **Total Area:** 431 km²
- **Total Population:** 281,968
- **Population Growth:** 0.36%
- **Unemployment Rate:** 10.7%
- **GDP:** $5.53 billion
- **GDP per capita:** $19,700
- **GDP growth rate:** 4%

SETTLEMENTS STRUCTURE

- **Capital City:** Bridgetown
  98,900 pop
- **Second City:** Speightstown
  3,651 pop
- **Density:** 654 pop/km²
- **Urban Population:** 53%

Political and administrative organisation
Constitutional monarchy with a parliamentary democracy composed of 11 parishes, and 5 development control areas for administrative purposes.

Administrative competence for planning
The Town and Country Development Planning Office is in charge of national planning. The Minister and/or the chief planner have total control over whether and where development will be permitted under the Development Order 1972.

Main planning legislation
The Town and Country Planning Act 1965 is based on the 1947 British Town and Country Planning Act which defined 'development', encompassing operations, infrastructure, change of use of land or buildings, and subdivision of land. The Town and Country Planning Development Order 1972 controls all land except the Scotland district.

Planning and implementation instruments
The planning system in Barbados contains three key components: a development planning system; a development control system and an enforcement system. The national physical development plan (NPDP) prescribes the overall national land use policy.

Development control
The Development Order prescribes that no development shall be undertaken upon any land in Barbados without the Permission of the Chief Town Planner or the Minister and it further requires that such permission can only be obtained on an application made in respect of the proposed development.

Planning system in practice
The planning system as a mechanism to guide development is constrained by the fact that the development planning process continues to lag significantly behind the actual development process. The proactive role of planning needs to be triggered by a planning system that is driven by the development plan process and there is an urgent need to have the system re-organised to incorporate this strategic and integrative role into the development process. There is a need for greater transparency in the planning process, and for increasing the opportunities of public participation. Appeals procedures are very restricted and participation in plan making non existent. There remains a great gap between planning and development and a need to attribute greater importance to the protection of nature, pollution control and the inclusion of environmental assessment in the planning process.

Read on: www.townplanning.gov.bb; www.barbados.gov.bb/govt.htm

FAST FACTS

- **Total Area:** 51,100 km²
- **Total Population:** 4,195,914
- **Population Growth:** 1.388%
- **Unemployment Rate:** 5.5%
- **GDP:** $55.95 billion
- **GDP per capita:** $13,500
- **GDP growth rate:** 6.1%

SETTLEMENTS STRUCTURE

- **Capital City:** San Jose
  337,200 pop
  1,527,300 (metro. area)

- **Second City:** Alajuela
  717,000 pop

- **Density:** 82 pop/km²

- **Urban Population:** 62%

Political and administrative organisation
Republic composed of 7 provinces, 81 provinces and 377 districts.

Administrative competence for planning
Institutions with competences in planning are diverse, not only in their activities but in their hierarchy, such as the National Institute of Housing and Urbanism, several Ministries - National Planning and Economic Politics; Environment and Energy; Public Works and Transportation) and the municipalities.

Main planning legislation
There is an ample legal base: National Planning Law; Urban Planning Law; Native Reserve Law; Statutory Law of Environment Wild Life; Conservation Law; Land and Colonisation Law; Law of Biodiversity and Law of Conservation and Use of Agricultural Land.

Planning and implementation instruments
Instruments vary according to different territorial scales. The national urban development plan constitutes the framework of spatial urban development. The national council for urban planning was set up to deal with widespread urban decay and provides the umbrella for the coordination of regional and urban development strategies. Regional plans are drawn up for specific territories (river basins, protected zones); municipal master plans and detailed plans are prepared for districts and neighbourhoods.

Development control
The limited technical and economic capacity of the local government reduces their capacity to control building activities and urban development, but training is provided through cooperation with the European Union.

Planning system in practice
The existing legal base for territorial planning often present overlaps, conflicts, duplication of competences and some vacuums while the planning system is still unknown by a large part of the population, and even the administration. The National Institute of Housing and Urbanism has been losing its capacity because of lack of adequate equipment and personnel. The municipalities, with some exceptions, do not have the resources to produce plans. The implementation of urban projects is slow, mainly due to the incapacity of the decision makers to conceptualise high-priority projects, the politicisation of urban issues, lack of agreements among partners and corruption, all problems that the country has been facing for many years. Its cooperation with the European Union on the plan for the metropolitan area of the capital, San Jose provides an opportunity for local staff to obtain training in planning and urban management. Also, municipalities resort increasingly to private consultants to assist them in their planning tasks. However the lack of resources and competence led to unsatisfactory results.

Read on: www.invu.go.cr; www.mideplan.go.cr; www.mopt.go.cr; www.ifam.go.cr; www.uinteramericana.edu; www.colegiodearquitectoscostarica.com;

FAST FACTS

- **Total Area:** 21,040 km²
- **Total Population:** 7,066,403
- **Population Growth:** 1.679%
- **Unemployment Rate:** 6.6%
- **GDP:** $35.97 billion
- **GDP per capita:** $5,200
- **GDP growth rate:** 4.7%

SETTLEMENTS STRUCTURE

- **Capital City:** San Salvador
  504,700 pop
  1,791,700 (metro. area)
- **Second City:** Santa Ana
  167,200 pop
- **Density:** 336 pop/km²
- **Urban Population:** 60%

Political and administrative organisation
Republic composed of 14 provinces (departmentos) and 262 municipalities.

Administrative competence for planning
Only the national level - Vice Ministry of Housing and Urban Development - and the local level – municipalities - are operational and deal with urban development processes.

Main planning legislation
There are several national laws. The Law of Urbanism and Construction 1955 gives the central government the capacity to carry out national planning. The Municipal Code 1987 enables municipal governments to elaborate urban and rural development plans. The Law of Territorial Development and Planning for the San Salvador Metropolitan Area 1993 focuses on the capital and the National Territorial Development and Planning Policy is in process of preparation. There is also an Environmental Law 1998 and other legislation affecting physical planning.

Planning and implementation instruments
The most recent and relevant plans are the master development plan for San Salvador metropolitan area and the San Andrés valley plan, 2000. The national territorial development plan, 2004 proposes strategic infrastructure for the whole country as well as a vision of optimum use and management of resources. It also proposes planning regions for projects of strategic importance. The urban plans for the four major cities have limited implementation capacity.

Development control
Any urban development, land subdivisions, and construction needs the approval of the local administration - if the project is located in a municipality which has an urban development plan – or of the national government, in consultation with local governments, if the municipality has no plan. Environmental assessments are also necessary.

Planning system in practice
Planning practice is limited due to the coexistence of several facts, among them, the obsolescence of the laws; the poor coordination between national and local institutions; the lack of specialised personnel; the absence of legal support to force private actors to follow planning guidelines; the incoherence between institutions which results in contradictory permits and resolutions given to private actors to undertake the development process; and lack of relations between local governments and civil society. None of the plans have been turned into statutory instruments which discredits the planning system. Nevertheless some actions, such neighbourhood planning which is widespread and successful in San Salvador, and the San Andrés's valley plan appear to be steps in the right direction. The problems derived from informal settlements still need to be regulated. A national spatial strategy and public private partnerships with the active involvement of the inhabitants are considered key conditions to achieve better housing conditions for all.

Read on: www.mop.gob.sv/ivvi.php; www.marn.gob.sv; www.upes.edu.sv;

63

GUATEMALA

FAST FACTS

- **Total Area:** 108,890 km²
- **Total Population:** 13,002,206
- **Population Growth:** 2.11%
- **Unemployment Rate:** 3.2%
- **GDP:** $67.45 billion
- **GDP per capita:** $5,400
- **GDP growth rate:** 5.6%

SETTLEMENTS STRUCTURE

- **Capital City:** Guatemala City
  1,128,800 pop
  2,655,900 (metro. area)
- **Second City:** Mixco
  287,600 pop
- **Density:** 119 pop/km²
- **Urban Population:** 47%

Political and administrative organisation
Republic composed of 8 regions, 22 provinces (departmentos) and 331 municipalities.

Administrative competence for planning
Each municipality is an autonomous institution in charge of territorial planning in its jurisdiction. As there is no regional government, the governors of the departments have to coordinate regional policies that will be reported directly to the President.

Main planning legislation
The main general laws that have a relationship to spatial planning are the Political Constitution, the Municipal Code, the Councils of Urban and Rural Development Law, the Civil Code and the Urban Subdivision Law, together with a Preliminary Urban Planning Law. Municipalities can devise their own regulations.

Planning and implementation instruments
Territorial plans are the exclusive competence of the municipality. The municipal code regulates the coordination of policies among municipalities and gives the municipalities the possibility to create 'municipality unions' to devise and implement common public policies, such as public transportation, drinking water, waste disposal, water treatment and environmental policies.

Development control
Land use, building and land subdivision must get special licences and approvals from the municipality. Local regulations usually include incentives for investors to obtain desired conditions in their projects, such as a better urban image, improved living conditions, and conservation of natural resources and the environment. Incentives may include tax and license fee reductions and time reduction of certain procedures.

Planning system in practice
Planning legislation is general and vague. Territorial regulations are not hierarchical and municipalities do not need state approval of their plans and regulations. There is a lack of specific rules to draw up and implement plans. Poverty, lack of housing, infrastructure and public facilities, migration to the main cities, environmental problems and corruption are the main problems for municipalities in dealing with planning. However, the municipalities with higher levels of growth have undertaken long-term planning policies in order to generate sufficient facilities, housing, employment, commerce, and transportation in their communities, all of them aspects that ought to assure a higher quality of life. Clearer, more integrated planning regulations developed with the participation of the inhabitants should prepare the ground for a more sustainable use of land and natural resources, better living conditions and a better balance between urban and rural development.

Read on: www.segeplan.gob.gt; http://ceur.usac.edu.gt; www.guatemala.gob.gt

FAST FACTS

- **Total Area:** 112,090 km²
- **Total Population:** 7,639,327
- **Population Growth:** 2.024%
- **Unemployment Rate:** 27.8%
- **GDP:** $30.65 billion
- **GDP per capita:** $4,100
- **GDP growth rate:** 6,3%

SETTLEMENTS STRUCTURE

- **Capital City:** Tegucigalpa
  1,248,300 pop
  1,436,000 (metro. area)
- **Second City:** San Pedro Sula
  385 000 pop
- **Density:** 68 pop/km²
- **Urban Population:** 46%

Political and administrative organisation
Republic composed of 18 provinces (departmentos) and 298 autonomous municipalities.

Administrative competence for planning
The National Board for Territorial Organisation is in charge of national planning. Since 1997 there has been a process of decentralisation transferring planning competences to the municipalities and making them the key administrative level for urban and territorial organisation.

Main planning legislation
The devastating effects of hurricane Mitch in 1998 proved the importance of having appropriate instruments for land use regulation and control. The Territorial Planning Act 2004 provides the legal basis for future national spatial organisation. However, no law is specifying the physical planning system and its instruments yet.

Planning and implementation instruments
Since the Territorial Organisation Act has not been developed yet, the plans in practice are the national development plan and the strategic municipal development plans (PEDM), most of which have been drawn up, validated and certified. In the wake of the hurricane the international donor community was assisting the country to reconstruct and transform its physical and administrative structures, including greater decentralisation and measures to reduce poverty. Local development planning and management is considered an essential means to contribute to this effort.

Development control
According to the Territorial Organisation Law, all territorial changes are subject to municipal planning. When the ordinances are not observed, the local government could impose heavy fines, including an order to pull down illegal constructions.

Planning system in practice
There is a real effort to make planning more participatory and responsive to local needs. It is embedded in fiscal sanctions and throughout the planning process assisted by a facilitator who produces concrete projects, implementation procedures and secures financing in an annual operational programme. Most municipalities have prepared their municipal strategic development plans, but their spatial and distributional aspects are weak because organisations in charge of this are not yet operative. Although the process of preparation of the PDEM is recent and only a small part of its contents has been realised, the municipalities are becoming aware of the importance of planning for their economic, social, cultural and environmental development. At the urban level, lack of controls and scarce municipal resources encourage the violation of regulations. Uncontrolled constructions have created incompatible uses and a shortage of open spaces and leisure areas.

Read on: www.soptravi.gob.hn; http://amhon.hn; www.serna.gob.hn;
www.usps.edu; www.e-cah.org

FAST FACTS

- **Total Area:** 5,128 km²
- **Total Population:** 1,047,366
- **Population Growth:** -0.891%
- **Unemployment Rate:** 6%
- **GDP:** $22.93 billion
- **GDP per capita:** $21,700
- **GDP growth rate:** 5.5%

SETTLEMENTS STRUCTURE

- **Capital City:** Port-of-Spain
  45,300 pop
  263,800 (metro. area)
- **Second City:** San Fernando
  56,000 pop
- **Density:** 204 pop/km²
- **Urban Population:** 76%

Political and administrative organisation
Republic composed of 9 regions, 3 boroughs and the cities of Port of Spain and San Fernando.

Administrative competence for planning
The Town and Country Planning Division is in charge of the preparation of development plans at the national, regional and local levels.

Main planning legislation
The Town and Country Planning Act 1969 established a comprehensive legal framework for physical development planning. Related legislations are the Environmental Management Act which provides measures for the protection of the environment, the Regional Corporation Act regulates the planning powers of the lower tiers, the Municipal Act defines health and safety measures, and Regulations exist on roads, water supply and disposal, drainage and fire prevention.

Planning and implementation instruments
The national physical development plan (NPDP) is the top planning level based on an integrated and comprehensive approach. Development plans at the regional and local levels are also prepared by the national Town and Country Planning Division and are supposed to fit into the NPDP framework. The private sector can prepare and propose development plans and they can be incorporated in local plans.

Development control
Development control is administered by the Town and Country Planning Division. Any person or entity has to apply for, and obtain permission before undertaking any form of development. Legal permission is granted, on application, by the responsible Minister, however the professional, technical and administrative work is done by the Town and Country Planning Division.

Planning system in practice
The planning system is highly centralised. There is provision in the law for the minister of government to delegate power to local government bodies but it has not been used so far. This contradicts the stated strategy to promote dispersed concentration of settlement development. The town and country planning division has become known as the administrator of the development control function. Any development control is often seen in a negative light because it is interpreted as a function which constrains or prevents persons from carrying out development. However, despite government incentives for growth pole development which is directed to the most dynamic cities and regions, the main constraint of planning is lack of implementation. Powerful developers obtain the agreement of the government even in contradiction with existing plans which the minister has approved. Thus, there is a growing understanding among the public of the need for stronger intervention by planners and the development control system as a lot of illegal development takes place regardless of plans, especially in inappropriate locations which includes the fringes of the already overcrowded capital.

Read on: www.planning.gov.tt; http://sta.uwi.edu

ARGENTINA

FAST FACTS

- **Total Area:** 2,766,890 km²
- **Total Population:** 40,677,348
- **Population Growth:** 0.917%
- **Unemployment Rate:** 8.9%
- **GDP:** $523.7 billion
- **GDP per capita:** $13,000
- **GDP growth rate:** 8.5%

SETTLEMENTS STRUCTURE

- **Capital City:** Buenos Aires
  2,768,772 pop
  13,349,000 (metro. area)
- **Second City:** Córdoba
  1,486,200 pop
- **Density:** 15 pop/km²
- **Urban Population:** 91%

Political and administrative organisation
Federal Republic composed of 23 provinces, 503 departments and 1 Federal District (Autonomous City of Buenos Aires)

Administrative competence for planning
There is no planning competence at national level. However, a series of studies at national level were instrumental in determining the existing sectoral national policies related to construction and national infrastructure. Other legislation land use bills were proposed in the 1980s but not adopted. The Ministry of Federal Planning, Public Investment and Services is in the process of developing several instruments, mainly the national system for territorial development and planning; the strategic territorial plan; the system of information and assistance for territorial development and planning, together with the required legal and normative framework. Provincial administrations have the competence for land use planning. Local authorities are responsible for regulating urban land use. The provincial constitutions make it possible to create metropolitan areas.

Main planning legislation
There is no national planning legislation. However, sectoral laws exist on cadastral issues, agriculture, and the environment. Specific national controls are set out on narrow coastline strips, interior lakes and main rivers, as well as areas of natural and cultural heritage and international boundaries. Buenos Aires is the only province which has approved its land use legislation; the remaining provinces apply only the existing sectoral legislation.

Planning and implementation instruments
The key instruments of planning consist of master plans and planning and building codes, yet only few cities have devised these planning instruments and they are non existent in rural areas. With the disappearance of the welfare state, the planning and development control capacities of local authorities were weakened.

Development control
Building and sectoral activities require municipal authorisation according to local ordinances. However, illegal land occupation and building are current activities.

Planning system in practice
Although Argentina does not have an integral planning legislation, there are some positive new proposals Planning exists only in political, social and professional discourses; there is no planning process and market forces are shaping the cities. There is a lack of relationships among the different administrative levels. Very few administrative bodies have specific planning units. Instead of being pro-active, the existing plans adopt existing tends. From 2000 there is a change towards the production of Local Development Plans. Public participation is slow in developing and it is not legally linked to administrative procedures.

Read on: www.minplan.gov.ar; www.ambiente.gov.ar; www.cnvivienda.org.ar; www.fadea.org.ar; www.cpau.org; www.aapur.com.ar; www.socearq.org; www.arq.unne.edu.ar

BOLIVIA

FAST FACTS

- **Total Area:** 1,098,580 km²
- **Total Population:** 9,247,816
- **Population Growth:** 1.383%
- **Unemployment Rate:** 8%
- **GDP:** $39.78 billion
- **GDP per capita:** $4,400
- **GDP growth rate:** 4%

SETTLEMENTS STRUCTURE

- **Capital City:** Sucre, 204,200 pop, La Paz, 830,500 pop, 1,576,100 (metro. area)
- **Largest City:** Santa Cruz 1,168,700 pop
- **Density:** 8 pop/km²
- **Urban Population:** 64%

Political and administrative organisation
Republic divided into 9 provinces (departamentos) and 311 municipalities.

Administrative competence for planning
The Ministry of Sustainable Development and Environment; through the National Planning Secretary, is in charge of the SISPLAN (Planning National System) which includes all administrative levels: national, provincial and local. Although municipalities are empowered by law with spatial development in their areas, the planning system is top down and hierarchical with arbitration vested at national level.

Main planning legislation
The Governmental Administration and Control Act 1990 has created SISPLAN. The Popular Participation Act 1994 encourages bottom-up planning process, and the Administrative Decentralisation Act 1995 devolves some powers to the local authorities.

Planning and implementation instruments
The SISPLAN mentions three territorial planning instruments: the executive plan and the regulatory plan for urban issues; and the territorial organisation plan for regional issues. The latter includes two types of plans: plans for land use (PLUS), according to the regional weaknesses and strengths, and territorial occupation plans (PLOT), to stimulate the regionalisation processes.

Development control
Municipalities can authorise planning changes to cope with the urban dynamics, i.e. increase of the number of floors in commercial and office areas; authorisation to build on municipals reserve plots or on inadequate plots, inclusion of rural lands for urban expansion. Municipalities can launch municipal ordinances for amnesty to legalise illegal plot division or buildings. Local organisations, such us the grassroots organisation - OTBs - are important agents for the promotion of neighbourhood upgrading.

Planning system in practice
After only a short time of implementation, SISPLAN recognises its deficiencies. The intended bottom-up process is jeopardised by the existing top-down decision-making process. Also, planning is linked to political election periods, as well as to sectoral political interests. Conversley, the planned public participation is mainly confined to local issues and not the planning process as such. The intended integrative nature of spatial planning with economic, social and environmental requirements has not yet materialised. Linkages are weak between the administration and society and among different levels of administrations. The high demand of urban land makes the municipal governments react against plans. The intended participatory planning is deficient and the transformation of the planning model is more theoretical than practical.

Read on: www.rds.org.bo; www.planificacion.gov.bo; www.uajms.edu.bo; www.ucb.edu.bo; www.cebem.org

BRAZIL

FAST FACTS

- **Total Area:** 8,511,965 km²
- **Total Population:** 191,908,598
- **Population Growth:** 0.98%
- **Unemployment Rate:** 9.8%
- **GDP:** $1.838 trillion
- **GDP per capita:** $9,700
- **GDP growth rate:** 4.5%

SETTLEMENTS STRUCTURE

- **Capital City:** Brasília
  2,160,100 pop
- **Second City:** São Paulo,
  10,927,985 pop,
  18,333,000 (metro. area)
- **Density:** 23 pop/km²
- **Urban Population:** 84%

Political and administrative organisation
Federal Republic composed of 26 States and one Federal District, and 5,564 municipalities.

Administrative competence for planning
The three levels of governance, federal, state and municipal, are autonomous and have powers to draw up and approve laws, decrees and plans, but legislation and ordinances of the three levels have to be compatible between them. They can also raise taxes and collect fees. At federal level, urban affairs are the responsibility of the Ministry of Cities, created in 2004. Other federal bodies affecting planning are the Secretary of the Interior and the Ministry of Integration. At state level, the Secretary for Planning or Urban Development, together with the municipalities, is responsible for local public policies. Municipalities are the entities with the capacity and responsibility to regulate and promote urban development in their jurisdiction.

Main planning legislation
Federal Law 10257, 2001, known as the "Statute of the City"; establishes directives for urban policy in the country. Other related provisions are the Federal Law of Urban Land Subdivision 1979, the Federal Constitution 1988, the Resolutions of the National Council for the Environment, and the Civil Code 2002.

Planning and implementation instruments
The federal constitution makes spatial planning compulsory. City planning is an obligation of the state to be implemented by the municipalities of over 20,000 inhabitants through different instruments: master plans; designation of built up areas, land subdivision and zoning laws, and building regulations. The Council of Cities lays down the content of local plans including local economic and social development goals. Responsibilities for the preservation of cultural heritage and the environment are joint responsibilities of all planning levels. Public participation is embedded in planning legislation.

Development control
Master plans must deal with urban property, building control, protection of historic sites and the natural environment, accessibility to services, besides strategies of spatial, economic and social development.

Planning system in practice
The 1988 Constitution strengthened the role of municipalities while weakening supra-local levels (states and metropolitan regions). The "Statute of the City" established new legal instruments and amplified the role of the municipality in controlling urban land use. However, many municipalities do not internalise the idea of the plan as a management tool, while community participation is limited. Local building and urban standards, frequently based on international norms, are beyond the economic capacity of many people, thus giving rise to widespread informal developments, especially on the outskirts of large cities.

Read on: www.planejamento.gov.br; www.mma.gov.br; www.fau.ufrj.br;
www.ufrgs.br; www.anpur.org.br; www.iabrj.org.br; www.cebrap.org.b;

CHILE

FAST FACTS

- **Total Area:** 756,950 km²
- **Total Population:** 16,454,143
- **Population Growth:** 0.905%
- **Unemployment Rate:** 7%
- **GDP:** $234.4 billion
- **GDP per capita:** $14,400
- **GDP growth rate:** 5.2%

SETTLEMENTS STRUCTURE

- **Capital City:** Santiago
  4,372,800 pop
  5,333,100 (metro. area)
- **Second City:** Viña del Mar
  303,100 pop
- **Density:** 22 pop/km²
- **Urban Population:** 88%

Political and administrative organisation
Republic composed of 13 regions, 51 provinces and 336 communes.

Administrative competence for planning
Except for the provinces, the state, the regions and the communes have their own planning instruments. The state has delegated the planning competences to the regional and communal level. Each region has a Regional Secretariat of the Ministry of Housing and Town Planning (SEREMI-MINVU). Each commune with cities of more than 40,000 inhabitants has its own Directorate of Public Works with Planning Consultants carrying out the planning work.

Main planning legislation
The Town Planning and Buildings General Law lays down the content and competences of planning among the administrative levels. It was preceded by the first National Planning Act in 1931 after a severe earthquake. The general law is complemented by the Town Planning and Buildings General Ordinance, amended in 1992. The Law of Regional Governments 1993 consolidated the decentralisation process of the country.

Planning and implementation instruments
Planning is mainly concerned with the confines of urban and building areas, the size of cities and the roles of towns with more than 7000 inhabitants. They consist of a system of public spaces and functional homogeneous zones. There are normative prescriptions for building activities and the subdivision of land into urban plots: plot sizes, intensity of occupation, building location and construction conditions, as well as land and building uses.

Development control
Every action concerning urbanisation and building requires permits and approvals from the Municipal Directorate of Public Works. The strategic content of plans has to be approved by the state and the technical aspects by the respective planning levels.

Planning system in practice
There are contradictions and conflicts between the legal and technical contents of the functional and zoning approach of planning and the free-market forces which seeks constraint free access to development land. Thus all land is evaluated purely in terms of building conditions. Communal plans and ordinances lack feedback, monitoring or verifications of their initial goals and public participation is limited. There are widespread slums and homeless people especially in large cities. Due to the pressing needs of urbanisation land owners have an almost free hand in developing areas inside and beyond cities. Subsidised housing activity can ignore planning dispositions, as the market is the main force which regulates social housing production.

Read on: www.mideplan.cl; www.minvu.cl; www.cipma.cl; www.eclac.org

COLOMBIA ▬

FAST FACTS

- **Total Area:** 1,138,910 km²
- **Total Population:** 45,013,674
- **Population Growth:** 1.405%
- **Unemployment Rate:** 10.6%
- **GDP:** $320.4 billion
- **GDP per capita:** $7,200
- **GDP growth rate:** 6.5%

SETTLEMENTS STRUCTURE

- **Capital City:** Santa Fe de Bogotá
  7,185,889 pop
  7,594,000 (metro. area)
- **Second City:** Cali
  2,283,200 pop
- **Density:** 40 pop/km²
- **Urban Population:** 77%

Political and administrative organisation
Republic composed of 32 departments and 1,096 municipalities.

Administrative competence for planning
The state does not have any direct planning powers. All planning and development matters are devolved to the municipalities which are in charge of plan making and have the power to approve their own plans. The upper administrative tiers, competent for planning control are the Metropolitan Boards, the Territorial Planning Boards and the Regional Autonomous Corporation. All other matters are regulated at the municipal level, or in groupings of municipalities, mainly in urban agglomerations.

Main planning legislation
The Regional Planning Law, 1997, defines the contents of the planning system and designates the plan for spatial organisation (development plan) as the instrument which guides spatial, physical development and land uses.

Planning and implementation instruments
There are tree types of plans: spatial development plans, for municipalities and districts with a population of more than 100,000 inhabitants; basic spatial development plans for municipalities between 30,000 and 100,000 inhabitants, and spatial development outlines for municipalities with a population of less than 30,000 inhabitants. Other instruments are the structure plans and environmental plans. There are also provisions to plan suburban land and to protect specific areas for topographic, environmental or landscape reasons, or to create reserves for public infrastructure.

Development control
The urban regulations of the use, settlement and exploitation of buildling land are the following: structural regulations, to fulfil the objectives of the spatial development plan; general regulations concerning land use and intensity of use, and complementary regulations to outline actions and proceedings for short term development.

Planning system in practice
The Act 388/97 gave a novel concept to Colombian planning. Urban Improvement, does not only allow the Spatial Development Plan to establish building typologies, land uses and construction rates, but also to determine the value of land which may increase or decrease according to levels of improvement. However, the potential offered for urban improvement has not been fully exploited because appropriate regulation as lacking. The legislation should be clear to avoid conflicts which might cause financial disadvantages either for the municipalities or the land and property owners concerned and capital gains are shared and partly invested in common goods by law.

Read on: www.dnp.gov.co; www.minambiente.gov.co; www.igac.gov.co:8o8o; www. unalmed.edu.co; www.sogeocol.edu.co, www.javeriana.edu.co/Facultades/Arquidiseno

FAST FACTS

- **Total Area:** 214,970 km²
- **Total Population:** 770,794
- **Population Growth:** 0.211%
- **Unemployment Rate:** 9.1%
- **GDP:** $4.057 billion
- **GDP per capita:** $5,300
- **GDP growth rate:** 4.5%

SETTLEMENTS STRUCTURE

- **Capital City:** Georgetown
  227,700 pop
- **Second City:** Bartica
  11,159 pop
- **Density:** 4 pop/km²
- **Urban Population:** 39%

Political and administrative organisation
Republic composed of 10 administrative regions.

Administrative competence for planning
Development control, urban development and planning are executed by the Central Housing and Planning Authority (CHPA) at the Ministry of Housing. National and regional land use planning is performed by the Guyana Lands and Surveys Commission (GLSC) under the aegis of the president's office. Local bodies have limited planning competences.

Main planning legislation
The Town and Country Planning Act 1946 provides the statutory basis for the preparation and adoption of town planning schemes, and for zoning. The Housing Act 1948 gives the CHPA the authority to control development. The Local Democratic Organisations Act 1980 instituted the administrative units of the country. The Guyana Lands and Surveys Commission Act 1999 empowers the GLSC as the authority for national and regional land use planning.

Planning and implementation instruments
Planning has its origin in rural agricultural based land development schemes. There is no zoning enabling legislation nor well defined comprehensive zoning ordinances tied to the building permit and enforcement process. Approved town plans do not exist for most of the urban areas, and regional plans are only now being developed. The main existing planning instruments are development control standards to guide the issuing and review of building permits. Also the housing act empowers the DHPA with development control and approval of town plans or other development projects. Larger towns have the powers to subdivide land into building plots for housing.

Development control
The CHPA is the institution which oversees development control matters which are otherwise shared between the central and the local level. Residential buildings with less than three stories in urban areas are controlled by the municipalities alone. For areas which have an approved plan building applications can be assessed for compliance with the plan.

Planning system in practice
The Guyana Lands and Surveys Commission has prepared land use plans for each of the regions of the country. CHPA has prepared several town plans, including extensive public consultations. Two critical aspects can be identified: the concurrent jurisdiction of different institutions for regional planning and the lack of enabling legislation for regional planning, thus although plans are being drawn up and approved their implementation is not backed up by enforcement capability. Also the local level is lacking technical and professional competence to carry out its planning responsibilities adequately and for that reason the central authorities are carrying out local planning with some local consultation.

Read on: www.chpa.gov.gy; www.sdnp.org.gy; www.epaguyana.org

PARAGUAY

FAST FACTS

- **Total Area:** 406,750 km²
- **Total Population:** 6,831,306
- **Population Growth:** 2.39%
- **Unemployment Rate:** 11.4%
- **GDP:** $26.55 billion
- **GDP per capita:** $4,000
- **GDP growth rate:** 4.5%

SETTLEMENTS STRUCTURE

- **Capital City:** Asunción
  525,100 pop
  1,482,200 (metro. area)
- **Second City:** Ciudad del Este
  239,500 pop
- **Density:** 17 pop/km²
- **Urban Population:** 59%

Political and administrative organisation
Republic composed of 17 provinces (departamentos) and 225 municipalities. .

Administrative competence for planning
Two State Secretariats are involved in national territorial planning: the Technical Planning Secretariat (TPS) whose role is to devise indicative national plans, and the Environment Secretariat in charge of applying environmental regulations. The provincial governments (Departamentos governments) are responsible for formulating plans in accordance with the national plan. Municipalities are drawing up urban plans under compulsory ordinances.

Main planning legislation
There is no a specific legislation about physical planning but there is an ample set of sectoral plans affecting the territory, mainly related to environmental and agrarian issues. Legislation focuses on rural development and health and safety. Although Paraguay subscribes to a number of international agreements on climate change and Agenda 21, it is not adjusting its existing legislation to these new tasks which have an impact on physical development and controls.

Planning and implementation instruments
There is no specific national physical planning system, but there exists an economic and social strategic plan adopted in 2002 which refers to settlements, migration and local development. At national level the Technical Planning Secretariat is in charge of formulating development plans to deal with economic and social issues. Governments of municipalities and of departamentos are legally obliged to produce territorial and urban plans for their areas. They consist of urban and environmental development plans and economic development plans respectively to satisfy the requests of external financial assistance agencies.

Development control
The various public administrations have the power to control implementation of plans through urban regulations.

Planning system in practice
National plans show partial and intermittent implementation. Plans developed by the departamento governments have been few: only 5% of municipalities have some sort of norm to regulate urban land uses. Planning is not deep-rooted in institutional practice and there is a tradition of non compliance with the law. Plans are devised as an end in themselves and not as a management instrument. This leads to many problems: territorial imbalances; environmental pollution; lack of infrastructure and basic public services; chaotic public transport; illegal and informal occupations; depreciation of historical areas; disorganised urban growth fuelled by migratory waves and the real estate market; and inadequate public services coverage in terms of accessibility and quality. Such a scenario does little to generate interest and create opportunities for private investment.

Read on: www.stp.gov.py/index800.htm; www.arq.una.py; www.cpi.org.py

FAST FACTS

- **Total Area:** 1,285,220 km²
- **Total Population:** 29,180,899
- **Population Growth:** 1.264%
- **Unemployment Rate:** 11.4%
- **GDP:** $217.5 billion
- **GDP per capita:** $7,600
- **GDP growth rate:** 7.5%

SETTLEMENTS STRUCTURE

- **Capital City:** Lima
  7,029,928 pop
  8,180,000 (metro. area)
- **Second City:** Arequipa
  837,300 pop
- **Density:** 23 pop/km²
- **Urban Population:** 75%

Political and administrative organisation
Republic composed of 26 autonomous regions (departamentos), 125 provinces (included the province of Callao, composed of 1 district) and 1,828 autonomous municipalities (districts). Autonomous neighbourhood committees are also influential but do not have formal powers in municipal matters. The Decentralisation process is on-going.

Administrative competence for planning
The Vice-Ministry of Urban Development of the Ministry of Housing, Construction and Sanitation is in charge of the National Land Use Agenda. Regional governments are vested to develop regional land development plans while municipal land use planning can be developed by both, provincial and district municipalities.

Main planning legislation
Several laws exist at national level: New Regulation for the General Law of Urban Subdivisions 2005, the Modification of the Regulation for Land Management, the Urban Development and Environment Law 2004, and the 2002 Law of Boundaries and Territorial Organisation of Regions. Legislation varies at local level as regions and municipalities are empowered to draw up their own planning laws and regulations.

Planning and implementation instruments
Regional and urban governments have to prepare their own plans and present them to the population. There are several planning instruments: regional plans for regional land uses; local comprehensive development plans, including social, economic and environmental and physical aspects, drawn up mostly at the local level; local framework plans for guiding urban expansion, and local development plans for urban districts, together with land use and strategic plans. Municipalities are also in charge of coordinating sectoral development and incorporating utilities and infrastructure plans, some by the private sector, into their physical plans.

Development control
The formal urbanisation process of the city falls under the Law of Subdivisions that specifies the conditions of the urbanisation process in the country.

Planning system in practice
The existing planning legislation is complex and limited and planning instruments are not adequate to solve urban problems. Planning activities depends on different authorities. This generates lack of authority and confusion. The legislation is not fully respected and this is allowed by the governments for political reasons. The demand of land by the poor grows at a rate beyond the control of local authorities. The new legislation includes public participation in the process of allocation of municipal financial resources. However, the land occupation policy is still unclear and tolerates the illegal appropriation of land.

Read on: www.vivienda.gob.pe; www.inade.gob.pe; www.pucp.edu.pe

URUGUAY

FAST FACTS

- **Total Area:** 176,220 km²
- **Total Population:** 3,477,778
- **Population Growth:** 0.486%
- **Unemployment Rate:** 9.2%
- **GDP:** $37.05 billion
- **GDP per capita:** $10,700
- **GDP growth rate:** 7.2%

SETTLEMENTS STRUCTURE

- **Capital City:** Montevideo
  1,347,600 pop
  1,745,100 (metro. area)

- **Second City:** Salto
  99,072 pop

- **Density:** 18 pop/km²

- **Urban Population:** 93%

Political and administrative organisation

Republic composed of 19 provinces (departamentos). There is no municipal government and cities are governed directly by 'intendentes'. A special case is the capital Montevideo which has grown beyond its province of the same name into the neighbouring province.

Administrative competence for planning

At national level the National Directorate of Panning (DINOT), of the Ministry of Housing, Planning and Environment (MVOTMA) is in charge of National and Regional Plans. The departamentos have competences to produce and approve master plans. In reality, the sectoral national institutions draw up their own plans without much coordination and consultation of the national planning directorate. A typical example of sectoral plans overruling all other instances is the national forestry plan.

Main planning legislation

The Urban Centres Law 1946 is the main legislation which regulates urban development. The National Constitution of 1997 includes aspects concerning planning and the Departmentos Organic Law 1935 defines the competences for guiding urban development at the provincial level. National planning legislation has so far been rejected by the government.

Planning and implementation instruments

The only formal planning instrument are master plans. However, the city of Montevideo has found a means of devising plans in cooperation with Spain. However, it covers only the area within its province and thus cannot regulate the development process of the metropolitan area. Only building regulations control private development.

Development control

Departamento governments authorise land subdivision projects and building permissions. The ordinances are a very strong normative. With the establishment of the new comprehensive ministry major cities have been allocated tools to formulate urban plans.

Planning system in practice

Spatial planning practice has not been used systematically as a tool of territorial administration. At national level, sectoral plans are developed without any relation with the remaining national institutions or the local governments. Public and private initiatives are made in the context of market laws and for political periods. There have been isolated cases – cities and departmentos – whose plans were formulated and very few managed to pass through the legal approval procedures; some of them have been used as guides to local government's actions but they are frequently not used by the administrations. The city of Montevideo is the unique administration that has the technical capacity to drawn up and implement its planning tools. There is a need to implement communication policies to allow free and complete reciprocal information flows between planning authorities and society, including public and private organisations.

Read on: www.mvotma.gub.uy; www.farq.edu.uy; www.sau.org.uy

FAST FACTS

- **Total Area:** 912,050 km²
- **Total Population:** 26,414,815
- **Population Growth:** 1.498%
- **Unemployment Rate:** 9.1%
- **GDP:** $335 billion
- **GDP per capita:** $12,800
- **GDP growth rate:** 8.3%

SETTLEMENTS STRUCTURE

- **Capital City:** Caracas
  1,741,400 pop
  3,517,300 (metro. area)
- **Largest City:** Maracaibo
  1,854,300 pop
- **Density:** 29 pop/km²
- **Urban Population:** 88%

Political and administrative organisation
Federal Republic composed of 24 states, 335 municipalities and 1,084 parishes.

Administrative competence for planning
According to the new Constitution there is a vertical distribution of the authority from the municipal, to the state and the national powers, placing them in this order according to their proximity to the citizenship, as a model of "participatory democracy". Consequently, the competences for planning matters are shared between the three administrative levels: the National Commission for Territorial Planning, Ministry of the Environment; the state Planning Agencies, and the Urban Planning Municipal Offices.

Main planning legislation
The two main laws are the Planning Law 2001 concerning socio-economic development issues, and the Territorial Planning Law 2005 for national, regional and local physical planning. Related legislation is the Environment Law 1976, Decentralisation, the Delimitation and Transfer of Competences of Public Power Law 1993, the Local Councils and Public Planning Law 2002, the Municipal Power Law 2005 and the Participation Law.

Planning and implementation instruments
Despite democratic and participatory principles embedded in law, the planning process is top down. At the federal level there exists a statutory framework which needs to be address in the formulation of regional and urban policies and plans. Sectoral national plans, such as the environmental strategy, affect plans at different territorial levels, i.e. state development plans, regional development plans, and municipal development plans. Development certificates are subject to plans in force.

Development control
Any activity with spatial impacts should request and obtain a Constancy of Conformity of Use from the authorities in charge of regional planning control. Sanctions are regulated by law. For spontaneous urbanisations spatial planning legislation proposes urban progressive developments (UPD) aimed to improve and legalise these areas. All plans have to be submitted to public consultation.

Planning system in practice
Planning is considered a public function but the private sector and individual citizens are encouraged to take an active part in the development process including those who build their own homes. Although the new legislation solves some of the planning problems in Venezuela, others prevail: disconnection between plans and implementation, absence of explicit urban policies, lack of coherence between regional plans and development plans. In reality, planning organisation is top down, in contradiction with the principles and objectives of the laws. In practice the greatest urban developer is the self-builder who makes the city by occupying urban and non urban land illegally.

Read on: www.mpd.gob.ve; www.mvh.gob.ve; www.farq.edu.uy; http://urbe.arq.ucv.ve;

Asia & Pacific

MIDDLE EAST
Iran
Iraq
Israel
Saudi Arabia

CENTRAL ASIA
Bangladesh
India
Kazakhstan
Maldivas
Pakistan
Sri Lanka
Uzbekistan

EAST ASIA
China
Hong Kong
Indonesia
Japan
Philippines
Singapore
South Korea
Taiwan
Vietnam

**AUSTRALASIA
and PACIFIC**
Australia
New Zealand
Samoa

Asia and Pacific

FAST FACTS

- **Total Area:** 1,648,000 km²
- **Total Population:** 65,875,223
- **Population Growth:** 0.792%
- **Unemployment Rate:** 11%
- **GDP:** $852.6 billion
- **GDP per capita:** $12,300
- **GDP growth rate:** 4.3%

SETTLEMENTS STRUCTURE

- **Capital City:** Tehran
  7,796,257 pop
- **Second City:** Mashhad
  2,061,100 pop
- **Density:** 40 pop/km²
- **Urban Population:** 68%

Political and administrative organisation

Theocratic Islamic Republic composed of 25 administrative provinces, 195 governorships, 5001 districts, 612 cities and 1581 villages.

Administrative competence for planning

Ministry of Housing and Urban Planning and for a period the Ministry of Interior, under the President's direct competence are responsible for urban planning. Municipalities lost their planning competence with the Planning and Budgeting Organisation instituted in 1948, reinstated for the period of the second development plan 1955-62.

Main planning legislation

Urban Land Act. Act of Construction and Road Building. Specifications of conformity for the whole country imposing uniform Islamic indigenous architecture, including the preservation of historic buildings and urban environments.

Planning and implementation instruments

Master plans are designed by the Ministries also for cities. Local authorities have a limited role in planning. They are mainly in charge to ensure conformity with national performance specifications, establishing a national style of architecture, buildings and urban spaces. Plans do not accommodate economic, social or environmental objectives.

Development control

There is no particular mechanism of development control and thus development on the ground shows problems of incompatible land uses, including congestion and conflict between road and pedestrian traffic.

Planning system in practice

Rapid urbanisation has led to urban problems in economic, social and environmental terms. Land flight took place from the countryside to smaller cities. Like larger cities beforehand they started to face problems of densification and expansions into green field land which were not anticipated in their master plans. The nationalisation of large tracts of land has provided opportunities for large scale speculative projects. Cities are considered unsustainable from a purely ecological point of view and efforts are made to improve the urban environment and the quality of life in fast growing cities. Various economic regimes affected the urbanisation process differently, with periods of liberal private development contributing to urban sprawl, besides informal settlement growth on city fringes. In recent years, nationalisation of large tracks of land enabled developers to realise very large scale projects on vacant land which did not follow development plans, brought about congestion increase and did not supply much needed affordable housing. Densification of inner cities exacerbated incompatible land uses and peripheral growth continued informally, as the planning system is not effective enough to enforce plans and regulations.

Read on: www.parstimes.com/gov_iran.htm; www.bhrc.gov.ir; www.iust.ac.ir;
www.mporg.ir; www.siap.org

IRAQ

FAST FACTS

- **Total Area:** 437,072 km²
- **Total Population:** 28,221,181
- **Population Growth:** 2.562%
- **Unemployment Rate:** 18 to 30%
- **GDP:** $100 billion
- **GDP per capita:** $3,600
- **GDP growth rate:** 5%

SETTLEMENTS STRUCTURE

- **Capital City:** Baghdad
  6,777,300 pop
  6,777,300 (metro. area)
- **Second City:** Mosul
  1,791,600 pop
- **Density:** 65 pop/km²
- **Urban Population:** 67%

Political and administrative organisation
Republic composed of 18 provinces (governorates).

Administrative competence for planning
Very centralised planning with Ministries responsible for strategic, provincial, city and rural planning and housing, although devolution to the provinces, the Kurdistan region and Baghdad (special status) has started, albeit without adjusting legislation. Municipalities are in charge of implementing plans, while the capital is responsible for drawing up its own plans.

Main planning legislation
The Town Planning Ordinance 1939 and the Country Parks Ordinance 1976 are still operative. The Town Planning Board deals with all planning matters. Without a legal definition of town planning regulations, the Board has discretionary powers. Ordinances exist on Building, Conveyancing, Property and Housing.

Planning and implementation instruments
Various Ministries plan through governorates and at municipal level. They produce master plans, governorates structure plans and municipalities detailed and zoning plans. Baghdad produces land subdivisions. Enforcement mechanisms are weak and settlement development in rural areas is uncontrolled. There is no tradition of public participation and the current situation hampers fledgling attempts. Building codes are borrowed from Europe or the USA. New construction standards are being elaborated.

Development control
Municipalities carry out development control. Development permits are necessary for all types of development and change of land use. Land subdivision has to obtain approval from the municipality of the governorate.

Planning system in practice
The current situation in Iraq is seriously infringing the workings of the planning process. In the inherited planning system which may well change with political restructuring of the country excessive centralisation hampers local priorities, delays development and leads to non compliance with planning regulations. Political interference and selective curbing of already scarce resources, and land allocated as favours discredit the planning system further. Horizontal segregation of planning powers at the centre leads to lack of spatial development coordination. Plans focus exclusively on land use and lack implementation procedures, including prioritising and budgeting. Lack of a sense of belonging of stakeholders also thwarts the planning process, together with lack of trained staff. It can only be hoped that with regularisation of the political and administrative future the planning system will also be reformed to make a positive contribution to new conditions of reconstruction and development, taking into account both local needs and cultural heritage.

Read on: -no electronic information found.

ISRAEL

FAST FACTS

- **Total Area:** 20,770 km²
- **Total Population:** 7,112,359
- **Population Growth:** 1.713%
- **Unemployment Rate:** 7.6%
- **GDP:** $184.9 billion
- **GDP per capita:** $28,800
- **GDP growth rate:** 5.1%

SETTLEMENTS STRUCTURE

- **Capital City:** Jerusalem
  695,500 pop

- **Second City:** Tel-Aviv
  365,300 pop

- **Density:** 342 pop/km²

80 • **Urban Population:** 92%

Political and administrative organisation
Parliamentary democracy composed of 6 administrative districts.

Administrative competence for planning
A three tier system of planning boards with politicians and professional representatives is responsible for planning: the national board for policies, public infrastructure and buildings, district boards for outline schemes, local boards for main statutory planning functions and development control.

Main planning legislation
The Planning and Building Law 1965, and some 50 amendments, most importantly in 1995, was modelled on the 1936 Town Planning Act under British Mandate.

Planning and implementation instruments
The Ministry of the Interior operates through the National Planning and Building Board. Planning Boards at national, district and local levels, as well as special boards and commissions for infrastructure, the preservation of coastal areas in the Mediterranean and open spaces (but less agricultural land) are in charge of planning strategies and approval. They include representatives of the building professions, private sector and civil society. National spatial strategies are approved by the government cabinet. Structure, district and local master plan approvals are carried out by the tier above hierarchically, except for some local plans. Licenses to build are issued by the Local Building Commission. Detailed plans are initiated by developers and/or landowners.

Development control
By laws define development control procedures and standards implemented by bodies designated by the Planning and Building Law.

Planning system in practice
The planning system is considered too rigid, centralised and top down covering all areas. Central planning powers were increased with the coastal protection law. although desalination and gas exploration goes ahead. Central powers have also enabled new settlements to occur on disputed land increasing disparity in the quality of the built environment. Licensing for private sector initiatives are long drawn out, but the law on infrastructure provision managed to speed up that part of the development process. The planning system is increasingly encompassing economic issues, property rights and added value of schemes provided by the public sector which benefit also private sector investment. With increased pressure on land by urban population growth protection of land ownership and property rights assumes a more central role to the grief of environmentalists who also oppose excessive transport infrastructure provision, desalination plants and exploration works for natural gas in the Mediterranean.

*Read on: www.moch.gov.il; http://sviva.gov.il; http://architecture.technion.ac.il/index.php;
www.isala.org.il; www.environment.tau.ac.il*

SAUDI ARABIA

FAST FACTS

- **Total Area:** 2,149,690 km²
- **Total Population:** 28,161,417
- **Population Growth:** 1.945%
- **Unemployment Rate:** 13%
- **GDP:** $572.2 billion
- **GDP per capita:** $20,700
- **GDP growth rate:** 4.7%

SETTLEMENTS STRUCTURE

- **Capital City:** Riyadh
  3,724,100 pop
- **Largest City:** Jeddah
  2,745,000 pop
- **Density:** 13 pop/km²
- **Urban Population:** 89%

Political and administrative organisation
Monarchy composed of 13 provinces, 14 amanats, 143 municipalities, 118 districts, 21 villages and 1,044 centres.

Administrative competence for planning
The King and the Council of Ministers appointed by him produce planning legislation. Ministries issue directives with implementation circulars. This three tier system of councils aims to incorporate citizens in the planning process and improve their quality of life. Members of regional councils are appointed by the Minister of Interior. Half of local council members are elected since 2005, the other half nominated by the minister of municipal and rural affairs. In 2005 the main municipality in each province became an Amanah instead of regional directorates in an effort of decentralisation.

Main planning legislation
Formal planning from 1930s selectively. In 1970 a formal town planning approach was adopted with physical emphasis. 2000 adoption of National Spatial Strategy. Model Land Development Code.

Planning and implementation instruments
Doxiadis´ plan for Riyadh in 1930s was a demonstration for initial planning. Masterplans were formulated for cities after 1970, and five year national sectoral plans. Quadrupling of oil prices in 1973 brought rapid urbanisation and infrastructure development with planning lagging behind. The mid 1980s produced comprehensive regional development plans controlling urban growth, countrywide public utilities strategies, city databases and a national spatial strategy for balanced development in 2000, followed by regional strategies. In 2005 all cities and village clusters obtained municipal councils with some responsibility for planning. Regional councils carry out regional planning coordination.

Development control
Strongly regulated development control is carried out at local level with central guidance.

Planning system in practice
The planning system remains a static process without follow up, evaluation or adjustment to fast changing circumstances. Lack of planning professionals prevents forward planning and concentrates activities on development control and procedural aspects. Planning excludes land management which undermines the pourpose of spatial planning. There is a need for a planning act and a spatial planning commission as ministries are considered as service providers, not in charge of spatial development. Thus planning at the national and regional level does not enjoy the support of other sectoral agencies. The centralised approach deprives regions and localities from taking into account site specific identity.

Read on: www.araburban.org; www.kfupm.edu.sa/crp

FAST FACTS

- **Total Area:** 144,000 km²
- **Total Population:** 153,546,901
- **Population Growth:** 2.022%
- **Unemployment Rate:** -
- **GDP:** $206.7 billion
- **GDP per capita:** $1,300
- **GDP growth rate:** 5.6%

SETTLEMENTS STRUCTURE

- **Capital City:** Dhaka
  5,378,023 pop
  12,560,000 (metro.area)
- **Second City:** Chittagong
  2,592,400 pop
- **Density:** 1,066 pop/km²
- **Urban Population:** 25%

Political and administrative organisation
Republic composed of 6 administrative divisions, 64 districts, 482 sub-districts, 4,484 unions and 85,650 villages.

Administrative competence for planning
The Ministries of Planning, Housing and Public Works, and Local Government, Rural Development and Co-operatives are involved in the regulation of the planning system. The latter has jurisdiction on the whole rural area of the country. A number of metropolitan development authorities have been established to prepare and implement master plans for some of the larger cities and urban areas. National economic planning is also entrusted in the ministry of planning which is responsible for public sector construction activities, urbanisation, city development and housing settlement aspects for the whole country. The jurisdiction of the Urban Development Directorate covers the whole urban area, with a few exceptions.

Main planning legislation
The Town Improvement Act 1953, as amended in 1987, made provision for the preparation of master plans. Local ordinances have established development authorities, town improvement trusts, development directorates and a capital development authority to prepare land use development plans. The Bangladesh National Building Code 2008 provides detailed guidance for all building activity.

Planning and implementation instruments
Although there is no national physical plan there are various economic sector plans. The development plans for the large urban areas consist of a structure plan which sets out a long-term growth strategy, and an urban area plan which provides a framework for the preparation of a detailed area plan.

Development control
The development and use of land is controlled by the appropriate urban authority, having regard to the provisions of the development plan in respect of land use, density and infrastructure provision.

Planning system in practice
The present planning system is both complex and diverse. This is in part due to the overlapping distribution of planning powers between central and local government and its needs streamlining. There is no national body for national physical planning and the metropolitan tier (region) is weak. The preparation of development plans and the exercise of planning control over the use and development of land is hampered by the shortage of professionally qualified planning staff and the many posts left vacant despite sufficient supply of qualified planners. Nevertheless, some improvement has taken place and both planners and citizens are putting pressure on the government to strengthen planning into an integrated system at national level. Dealing with recurrent natural disasters like flooding need particular attention.

Read on: www.plancomm.gov.bd; www.mohpw.gov.bd; http://bip.org.bd;
www.buet.ac.bd; www.kuurp.ac.bd

INDIA

FAST FACTS

- **Total Area:** 3,287,590 km²
- **Total Population:** 1,147,995,898
- **Population Growth:** 1.578%
- **Unemployment Rate:** 7.2%
- **GDP:** $2.965 trillion
- **GDP per capita:** $2,700
- **GDP growth rate:** 8.5%

SETTLEMENTS STRUCTURE

- **Capital City:** New Delhi
  9,817,439 pop
  15,334,000 (metro. area)
- **Largest City:** Mumbai
  11,914,398 pop
- **Density:** 333 pop/km²
- **Urban Population:** 29%

Political and administrative organisation
Federal Republic composed of 28 states, 7 union territories and over 550 districts.

Administrative competence for planning
The federal government formulates national policies, allocates the funds for planning and with the states enacts legislation for industrial growth, tourism, ecology and heritage. The states can enact legislation for regional and urban planning, land access, housing, slum up-grading and urban transport. The municipal authorities are empowered to prepare district plans.

Main planning legislation
The Municipal Acts made provision for the preparation of town planning schemes. State Town Planning Acts were adopted from 1914 onwards. The Central Slum Improvement Act 1956 shifted from slum clearance to slum improvement. The Constitutional Amendment Acts 1992 have transferred responsibility for dealing with public land disputes to local government.

Planning and implementation instruments
The complex hierarchy of development plans encompasses a 20 year state vision of national and regional policies, programmes and sectoral funds. The district planning committees prepare 20 year perspective development plans including development control rules. The municipal authorities prepare detailed plans.

Development control
Local authorities are required to strengthen their planning and development control regulations to include land sub-division, density, height and set back restrictions, as well as heritage and conservation.

Planning system in practice
The planning system is ill equipped to respond to the problems posed by land shortages, plan implementation and enforcement. After independence it was unable to regulate population growth but slum improvement should help. Physical planning and fiscal programmes are now integrated as opposed to uncoordinated sectoral public investment and segregation between spatial and socio-economic planning and fragmented public transport planning. Planning continues to control growth while the five year national programmes have shifted to ecological management. Despite a brown field site development policy at high densities, crisis planning dominates cities and their uncontrolla

Read on: http://pib.nic.in , www.nird.org , http://planningcommission.nic.in ,
www.spa.ernet.in , www.uni-mysore.ac.in , www.igidr.ac.in , www.cdsaindia.org ,

FAST FACTS

- **Total Area:** 2,717,300 km²
- **Total Population:** 15,340,533
- **Population Growth:** 0.374%
- **Unemployment Rate:** 7.3%
- **GDP:** $161.5 billion
- **GDP per capita:** $10,400
- **GDP growth rate:** 8.7%

SETTLEMENTS STRUCTURE

- **Capital City:** Astana
  288,200 pop
- **Largest City:** Almaty
  1,045,900 pop
- **Density:** 6 pop/km²
- **Urban Population:** 56%

Political and administrative organisation
Republic composed of 14 provinces (oblast), 160 districts, 85 cities, 10 municipal districts, 195 settlements and 150 rural counties or villages.

Administrative competence for planning
The central government is responsible for national spatial strategy. The Agency of Land Resource Management is overseeing planning legislation and coordinating sectoral inputs from other ministries. Provinces are competent for devising regional plans, their ratification and implementation. Cities and rural entities are the initiators of their master planning. There is also provision for urban planning of complex development projects, as well as in areas of special interest in which the provincial and the municipal levels are cooperating.

Main planning legislation
The Architectural, Town Planning and Building Activities in Kazakhstan Act 2001 was introduced after independence from the Soviet Union, together with the Land Code Act of the Republic of Kazakhstan 2003.

Planning and implementation instruments
The general national plan is guiding spatial and economic development. Local authorities at provincial, city and rural settlement levels are the initiators of plan making and changes. Producing master plans forms part of their budgeted activities carried out on request of the executive. Master plans are ratified and approved by the political executive. Private owners can initiate proposals on their land but need planning approval for their projects.

Development control
The appropriate level is in charge of its own development control, mainly the municipalities, except for areas of special interest. Private initiatives are possible, subject to approval in principle by relevant executive public bodies.

Planning system in practice
After the demise of the Soviet Union, the administrative structure which regulated the planning process and competences in Kazakhstan disappeared. This left a vacuum and led to a lack of coordination between sectoral development strategies. Currently, long term strategic planning is exposed to pressures from short term sectoral objectives and development tends to occur outside a coherent vision of spatial development. The state has to regain control of the overall spatial development process to secure a sustainable evolution of the country which is exposed to strong outside pressures due to its many underexploited primary resources such as oil and minerals. A national body is required to coordinate sectoral governmental planning organisations and regulate their spatial repercussions, together with a mechanism for public debate and more public participation.

Read on: www.world-newspapers.com/kazakhstan.html; www.undp.kz/script_site.html;
www.uskazakhstanchamberofcommerce.8k.com

FAST FACTS

- **Total Area:** 300 km^2
- **Total Population:** 379,174
- **Population Growth:** 2.69%
- **Unemployment Rate:** -
- **GDP:** $2.839 billion
- **GDP per capita:** $3,900
- **GDP growth rate:** 5.5%

SETTLEMENTS STRUCTURE

- **Capital City:** Malé
  81,600 pop
- **Second City:** U'ngoofaaru
  12,953 pop
- **Density:** 1,264 pop/km^2
- **Urban Population:** 30%

Political and administrative organisation
Republic composed of 21 administrative atolls, including the Male Urban Region.

Administrative competence for planning
In 1999 the president outlined the Maldives Vision 2020 which set out broad principles for the future development of the country. The Ministry of Planning and National Development is responsible for the preparation of national and regional development plans. The Ministry of Housing and Urban Development is responsible for issuing planning guidance, and the preparation and approval of land use plans.

Main planning legislation
At present there is no planning legislation, building legislation and building codes. There is a section in the Maldivian Land Law which stipulates that a land use plan should be prepared before any housing plots are allowed on uninhabited islands.

Planning and implementation instruments
The government is committed to the preparation of land use plans for the islands. In due course there will be a hierarchy of national, regional, urban area development plans and island land use plans. In 2005 the Ministry of Housing and Urban Development issued guidance on the preparation and implementation of development plans.

Development control
There is no formal system of development control and no need to obtain planning permission for development outside Male, Villingilli and Hulhumale. The Ministry of Housing and Urban Development is empowered to grant permission for the use of land without recourse to an island land use plan. Most single storey buildings do not require planning permission.

Planning system in practice
The planning system is still emerging and there are few regulations governing the preparation, form, content and approval of development plans. There is a wish to simplify the planning system which seems to be too complex for a small country with a small population. However, there does not seem an easy solution for the special geographic conditions of the country Coordination between the sectoral responsibilities at national level is lacking and this has adverse repercussions on spatial development and management of scarce resources. Land tenancy and management issues constitute a problem. The most important spatial development issue is whether to concentrate the populations on a few islands or leave them dispersed across the archipelago. Both options require new planning measures as the current situation is very inefficient and prolongs great disparity in living conditions.

Read on: www.planning.gov.mv; www.mv.undp.org

Political and administrative organisation
Federal Republic composed of 4 provinces, 26 divisions, 106 districts, 376 tehsils and 4,147 union councils.

Administrative competence for planning
The federal government, the provincial governments and local government are responsible for regional and urban planning. The government formulates the national planning framework and policies which are incorporated and articulated in the regional and urban plans prepared by the provincial authorities. The district authorities are responsible for the regulation of urban and rural settlements, the implementation of action area plans, and the exercise of building and planning controls.

Main planning legislation
Planning legislation at national, provincial and district levels is sporadic. There are numerous provincial planning acts, the earliest of which was passed in 1922 in the Punjab, together with a number of specific area ordinances. The statutory provisions for planning figure prominently in the ordinances which make provision for the reform of local government.

Planning and implementation instruments
The Federal Planning Commission prepares and implements the 20 year perspective plan, and the 5 year plans for the development of the country. These plans define the national spatial planning framework which informs the programmes prepared by the ministries responsible for socio-economic development, housing and environmental protection. The master plans, structure plans and outline development plans prepared by the provincial authorities develop these national policies. The district plans identify site specific policies, proposals and development control standards.

Development control
The plans prepared by the district, tehsil and union councils include zoning and building regulations to control the development and use of land. The present arrangements for enforcing these controls are weak, which results in many infringements of the planning and building regulations.

Planning system in practice
The present planning system focuses more on the physical than the socio-economic aspects of development. Planning tends to be considered as an aim in itself, thus implementation constitutes a problem. The regions tend to carry out comprehensive plans which have an overpowering influence over urban and local planning. Their aim is to establish better links between urban and rural areas and to incorporate socio-economic aims in an integrated spatial development strategy. Operational responsibility for planning also rests at provincial level and hampers coordinated action at the local level. Physical planning is overshadowing socio-economic strategies without coordination between sectors and levels of decision making.

Read on: http://202.83.164.26/wps/portal/Mohw5; www.uderc.com/index.html; www.pcatp.org.pk; www.uet.edu.pk

FAST FACTS
- **Total Area:** 803,940 km^2
- **Total Population:** 167,762,040
- **Population Growth:** 1.805%
- **Unemployment Rate:** 7.5%
- **GDP:** $446.1 billion
- **GDP per capita:** $2,600
- **GDP growth rate:** 6.3%

SETTLEMENTS STRUCTURE
- **Capital City:** Islamabad
  601,600 pop
- **Largest City:** Karachi
  9,339,023 pop
  11,819,000 (metro area)
- **Density:** 209 pop/km^2
- **Urban Population:** 35%

SRI LANKA

FAST FACTS

- **Total Area:** 65,610 km²
- **Total Population:** 21,128,773
- **Population Growth:** 0.943%
- **Unemployment Rate:** 6.3%
- **GDP:** $83.21 billion
- **GDP per capita:** $4,100
- **GDP growth rate:** 6%

SETTLEMENTS STRUCTURE

- **Capital City:** Colombo
  656,100 pop
  2,436,000 (metro. area)
- **Largest City:** Dehiwala- Mount
  Lavinia 214,300 pop
- **Density:** 322 pop/km²
- **Urban Population:** 21%

Political and administrative organisation
Socialist Republic composed of 9 provinces and 25 districts.

Administrative competence for planning
The government is responsible for the definition and operation of the planning system. The Technical Advisory Committee, the Inter-Ministerial Committee and the National Physical Planning Council are responsible for the preparation, approval and implementation of national policy. The National Physical Planning Board, the Urban Development Agency and the Board of Investment are responsible for different aspects of national, regional and local planning policy and plans.

Main planning legislation
The legislation passed in 1915 and 1946 established the basic physical planning framework and made provision for the preparation of planning schemes. Although it also empowered the Minister to issue national planning policy guidelines and to prepare regional plans these powers were not used. In 2000 the ordinance was amended to require the preparation and implementation of national physical planning policy guidelines.

Planning and implementation instruments
There is a hierarchy of national, regional and local planning instruments. The national planning policy for Sri Lanka has recently been prepared and it is currently in the process of obtaining the approval of the appropriate bodies. Several provincial plans have also been prepared in accordance with these national policy guidelines. Some local plans are being prepared, by the Urban Development Agency, for major townships and other urban areas designated by the Minister.

Development control
The hierarchy of plans provides the framework for controlling the development and use of land.

Planning system in practice
The complex procedures governing the preparation, approval and implementation of development plans and the hierarchic system constitute a problem, especially as there does not exist a clear definition of an urban area and there is confusion between municipal, urban and town councils and their respective competences. Plans do not only have to be approved vertically but also by a number of sectoral agencies. There is no integration between spatial and economic planning which are being pursued independently from each other. Despite a will to obtain equitable spatial development at regional level conceived as crucial for economic progress, the capital city region is dominating the settlement pattern and creating large disparities with the other regions. The complex planning procedures are difficult to implement as there is a lack of qualified professional planners at all levels.

Read on: www.priu.gov.lk/Ministries_2007/Min_Urban_Dev_Sacred_Area_Devpt.htm;
www.priu.gov.lk/Ministries_2007/Min_Housing_Common_amenities.html
www.mrt.ac.lk; www.mrt.ac.lk/tcp;

FAST FACTS

- **Total Area:** 447,400 km²
- **Total Population:** 28,268,440
- **Population Growth:** 1.753%
- **Unemployment Rate:** 0.8%
- **GDP:** $64.15 billion
- **GDP per capita:** $2,300
- **GDP growth rate:** 9.5%

SETTLEMENTS STRUCTURE

- **Capital City:** Tashkent
  2,155,400 pop
  3,457,500 (metro. area)
- **Second City:** Samarkand
  374,900 pop
- **Density:** 67 pop/km²
- **Urban Population:** 38%

Political and administrative organisation
Republic composed of 12 provinces, 1 city and 1 autonomous republic.

Administrative competence for planning
At a national level, planning considers the spatial organisation of the republic as a whole. An analysis of this focuses on both the patterns of movement and migration, as well as the structure of settlements and urbanisation. This informs regional planning focusing on economic growth and the parameters for development within each region. At local level, cities and other settlements produce plans aimed at transforming and improving the city environment, providing the strategic direction and regulating development for future 20-25 years.

Main planning legislation
Uzbekistan is currently writing new laws relating to town planning, and forming new standards to guide development and design. State policy in the field of town-planning is regulated by the Town-planning Code of the Republic of Uzbekistan.

Planning and implementation instruments
At a regional level, plans seek to guide economic development and land use within each particular province. At a more detailed level, local plans focus on the city structure, industrial development, zoning for development and land use, infrastructure, and the improvement of the natural environment. Although compulsory, plans are not produced for all cities due to costs and economic constraints.

Development control
Plans determine the content of development control exercised the local level where land use zoning is guiding development. There is a conflict between the need to conserve the older, historic areas of cities, and house an increasing urban population.

Planning system in practice
Since independence, the introduction of market attitudes in all fields of activity has resulted in significant changes in social and economic development. The planning system is therefore changing to respond to this. Planning in Uzbekistan could be improved through planning for different regions, and by encouraging the growth of smaller cities within regions. Historic areas within cities need to be protected, and new industrial development needs to be encouraged. Adequate recreational spaces, parks and open spaces within cities are often lacking. Communications and transportation linkages between regions and settlements, as well as infrastructure and access to basic services, need to be improved to create a better basis for more equitable settlement development and improve the position of smaller cities and towns. The capital continued to grow and produce urban sprawl.

Read on: www.gov.uz; www.press-service.uz; www.uzbekistan.org

FAST FACTS

- **Total Area:** 9,596,960 km²
- **Total Population:** 1,330,044,605
- **Population Growth:** 0.629%
- **Unemployment Rate:** 4%
- **GDP:** $7.043 trillion
- **GDP per capita:** $5,300
- **GDP growth rate:** 11.4%

SETTLEMENTS STRUCTURE

- **Capital City:** Beijing
  8,689,000 pop
- **Second City:** Shanghai
  10,996,500 pop
  12,665,000 (metro. area)

- **Density:** 139 pop/km²
- **Urban Population:** 41%

Political and administrative organisation
The Socialist Republic is composed of 23 provinces, 5 autonomous regions and a large number of autonomous prefectures, cities and communities.

Administrative competence for planning
The Government Ministries of Land, Natural Resources and Construction are responsible for urban planning and development. The Environmental Protection Agency formulates environmental policy and contributes to planning legislation. The provincial governments have similar powers. They are responsible for land administration, planning and construction. They control cities, except large cities which have their own urban and rural commissions and resettlement powers. Lower tier authorities have limited but sometimes relevant responsibilities. The state has the power to establish directly ruled special administrative areas.

Main planning legislation
The principal national town planning legislation includes the Environmental protection Law 1987, the City Planning Law 1989, the Urban Real Estate Administration Law 1994, and the Land Administration Law 1998. The provincial governments can adopt local planning laws subject to national legislation. New legislation is being prepared to accommodate changes to market mechanisms.

Planning and implementation instruments
The state prepares a 15 year national plan, with annual land use plans co-ordinating national socio-economic, environmental and cultural goals in spatial terms. The provincial governments prepare frameworks for city and local planning, including land classification of farm and development land. The cites prepare comprehensive plans and operational frameworks for detailed local plans which set out standards to be observed by developers, e.g. plot ratio, building height and site coverage.

Development control
They are administered jointly by the respective land administration and city planning departments. Developers have to obtain land use rights by the state usually by auction against a fee, as all land is in public ownership. Similar procedures exist for public use of land.

Planning system in practice
Growing concern at the complex inflexible nature of the planning system is addressed by the government. Yet, development takes place at an unprecedented pace, despite hurdles of switching to a demand led socialist market economy. Conflicting principles apply to the treatment of historic areas from occupied times while basic provisions of hygiene are lacking especially in rural areas. Rapid growth leaves declining areas in need of development corporations and public private partnerships to redress the growing disparity between developing and stagnating areas. Post modern design chaos and pollution tend to defeat the planning system.

Read on: www.cin.gov.cn , www.caupd.com , www.caup-tongji.org/wpsc2001

HONG KONG

FAST FACTS

- **Total Area:** 1,092 km²
- **Total Population:** 7,018,636
- **Population Growth:** 0.532%
- **Unemployment Rate:** 7.2%
- **GDP:** $293.4 billion
- **GDP per capita:** $42,000
- **GDP growth rate:** 5.8%

SETTLEMENTS STRUCTURE

- **Capital City:** Hong Kong
  986, 800 pop
- **Second City:** Kowloon
  2,070,000 pop
- **Density:** 6 pop/km²
- **Urban Population:** 93%

Political and administrative organisation
Special Administrative Region of the People's Republic of China composed of 18 administrative districts.

Administrative competence for planning
Several government agencies are responsible for the operation of the land use planning system. The Secretary for Housing, Planning and Lands oversees the operation of four departments; Building, Lands, Planning and Land Registry. The Town Planning Board deals with all planning matters and the Secretary for Environment, Transport and Works with public works.

Main planning legislation
The Town Planning Ordinance 1939 and the Country Parks Ordinance 1976 are still operative. Without a legal definition of town planning regulations, the Board has discretionary powers. Ordinances exist on Building, Conveyancing, Property and Housing.

Planning and implementation instruments
Like in China, all land in Hong Kong is legally owned by the government and offered for leasing at auctions. This enables the government to exert control over the use and development of the land when granting a development lease against a fee. The Planning Department prepares a hierarchy of land use plans including a Territorial Development Strategy, five Sub-regional Strategy Reviews, local land use and zoning plans and the Hong Kong planning standards and guidelines. The new vision for 2030 plans for Hong Kong as a part of China. Change of use is not regulated by statute but decided by the Building and Planning Authorities and commands a premium payment. The Urban Renewal Authority is in charge of improving the excising environment, including lowering densities.

Development control
The development control powers of the Lands department have gradually been replaced, displaced or duplicated by the Town Planning Board. Between them these bodies are responsible for granting planning permission for proposed development projects on scarce building land but land reclamation is being contested on environmental grounds.

Planning system in practice
Recently the Government has sought to amend the provisions of the Town Planning Ordinance with a view to strengthening and centralising the exercise of control over the development and use of land. 70% of Hong Kong is strictly controlled park land which increases land and property prices. Thus the property market forms an important part of Hong Kong's economy. The separation of planning powers into three agencies with the courts as final arbiters complicates the development process but acts against corruption. However, the government is taking measures to strengthen central control as land for housing, often in public ownership, is exempt from development control. For this purpose it weakens the lands department and passes powers to the town planning and building authorities which aim to streamline development with mainland China.

Read on: www.spcept.org , www.spcept.org , www.hkip.org.hk

INDONESIA

FAST FACTS

- **Total Area:** 1,919,440 km²
- **Total Population:** 237,512,355
- **Population Growth:** 1.175%
- **Unemployment Rate:** 9.7%
- **GDP:** $845.6 billion
- **GDP per capita:** $3,400
- **GDP growth rate:** 6.1%

SETTLEMENTS STRUCTURE

- **Capital City:** Jakarta
  8,389,443 pop
  13,194,000 (metro. area)
- **Second City:** Surabaya
  3,038,800 pop
- **Density:** 124 pop/km²
- **Urban Population:** 48%

Political and administrative organisation

Republic composed of 30 provinces, 348 regencies, 92 municipalities, 4,994 districts and 70,921 sub-districts.

Administrative competence for planning

The National Development Planning Board is responsible for the preparation and implementation of the national development plan, as well as the management of human and financial resources. The National Spatial Planning Coordinating Agency is responsible for the implementation of the national plan, and for monitoring and evaluating its outcomes. The Province Planning Board and the Regency Town Planning Board likewise monitor and evaluate the development outcomes with regard to their respective administrative powers and functions.

Main planning legislation

The National Development Planning System Ordinance 2004 defines the procedures for the preparation of long-range, medium-term and annual plans prepared by the central and local governments.

Planning and implementation instruments

National, regional and local plans provide the powers, procedures and framework for the exercise of planning control over the development and use of land in a hierarchic system, although development planning is approached simultaneously from the top down and bottom up. The national spatial strategy defines general principles of a development framework while the middle range development plans include regional and financial plans. The annual plans at regional and local levels are operational plans and include specific programmes and projects.

Development control

Public control is exercised over the development and use of land to ensure that it complies with the provisions of the hierarchy of national, regional and local plans.

Planning system in practice

Spatial planning includes a large number of sectoral objectives and is perceived to be too idealistic and thus difficult to implement. The spatial planning system needs to be more focussed on land management. Particular problems have arisen in respect of the provision and maintenance of infrastructure and public open space. There is still strong public sector support for the preparation of comprehensive spatial land use plans which provide a framework for the provision of basic infrastructure and much needed social capital. Physical planning tends to dominate as it is still supported by public sector investment which is the main driver of physical and economic investment. Thus implementation occurs to the detriment of environmental and social strategies despite official endorsement of sustainability principles.

JAPAN

FAST FACTS

- **Total Area:** 377,835 km²
- **Total Population:** 127,288,419
- **Population Growth:** -0.139%
- **Unemployment Rate:** 4%
- **GDP:** $4.417 trillion
- **GDP per capita:** $33,800
- **GDP growth rate:** 1.9%

SETTLEMENTS STRUCTURE

- **Capital City:** Tokyo
  8,483,050 pop
  35,327,000 (metro. area)
- **Second City:** Osaka
  2,597,000 pop
- **Density:** 337 pop/km²
- **Urban Population:** 66%

Political and administrative organisation
Constitutional monarchy composed of 10 planning regions, 47 prefectures and designated cities and 2,325 districts.

Administrative competence for planning
The Minister of Land, Infrastructure and Transport is responsible for national, regional and local planning. The Land Development Agency is responsible for preparing the Comprehensive National Development Plan. Each ministry has its own regional bureau covering several prefectures and their constituent municipalities. The local planning councils, which have been established in the prefectures, towns and cities are empowered to prepare, approve and implement land use plans.

Main planning legislation
The City Planning Law 1968 designated areas for urbanisation and contraction respectively and defined 8 land use categories. The Land Use Planning Law 1974 stipulated that state, prefecture and municipal land use plans should be prepared. The National Land Formation Plan Law 2005 abolished the Comprehensive National Development Plan reflecting a shift of emphasis from expansion to contraction.

Planning and implementation instruments
There is a hierarchy of national, regional and local plans. The national plans set out the government's goals, policy statements, and proposals for settlements, industrial location and transportation networks. The regional plans formulate strategies for settlements, industrial location and new towns. The city plans set out planning regulations and requirements, including planning policies for the control of land use, zoning controls, design control, plot ratio and density standards.

Development control
Municipal authorities have to ensure that proposed developments comply with the detailed provisions of the district plans. Developers have to obtain permission before undertaking plot sub-division and the construction of buildings.

Planning system in practice
The planning system is having to respond to the societal changes brought about by economic decline and population decrease. Population decrease is a major cause of change and this causes dysfunctions in existing towns and the surrounding areas which grew rapidly during economic expansion and had drained the town centres of their services. They have become inappropriate for the current socio-economic needs of an ageing society both in central and peripheral areas. Incentives are being offered to the private sector to stimulate decentralised growth. However, city centres including Tokyo are acquiring a new lease of life. With incentive zoning they attract people back to less congested inner city areas due to reduced overall demand.

Read on: www.mlit.go.jp/english/index.html , www.pcatp.org.pk, www.its.go.jp/ITS,

SOUTH KOREA

FAST FACTS

- **Total Area:** 98,480 km²
- **Total Population:** 49,232,844
- **Population Growth:** 0.371%
- **Unemployment Rate:** 3.2%
- **GDP:** $1.206 trillion
- **GDP per capita:** $24,600
- **GDP growth rate:** 4.9%

SETTLEMENTS STRUCTURE

- **Capital City:** Seoul
  10,287,847 pop
- **Second City:** Pusan
  3,504,900 pop
- **Density:** 500 pop/km²
- **Urban Population:** 81%

Political and administrative organisation
Republic composed of 9 provinces, the capital city Seoul, 6 metropolitan cities, counties and districts.

Administrative competence for planning
The Ministry of Construction and Transportation is responsible for the definition and implementation of national policies for land, housing, transportation, urban development, the environment, and the construction industry. These policies are set out in the Comprehensive National Territorial Plan. The regional plans are prepared by the provincial and metropolitan governments, and the local development plans are prepared by the municipal authorities to implement and enforce these policies.

Main planning legislation
The guiding principles and institutional framework of the planning system are formulated in the Land Use and Territory Act 2002. It sets out the procedures for the planning and use of the national territory, and establishes a hierarchy of national, regional and local land use plans. The Residental Land Development Promotion Act 1980 regulates housing provision.

Planning and implementation instruments
The comprehensive national territorial plan identifies long-range goals for the planning, use, development and protection of land. This national framework underpins the provincial comprehensive plans which identify each province's planning goals and development strategies. The urban structure plans prepared by the municipal authorities present their spatial policies for the distribution of population, open space, land uses, and the improvement of the natural environment.

Development control
The urban development plans prepared by the municipal authorities set out a range of measures such as land use and plot ratio zoning to regulate the development and use of land.

Planning system in practice
Growing concern at the complex inflexible nature of the planning system is addressed by the government. Yet, development takes place at an unprecedented pace, despite hurdles of switching to a demand led socialist market economy. Conflicting principles apply to the treatment of historic areas from occupied times while basic provisions of hygiene are lacking especially in rural areas. Rapid growth leaves declining areas in need to development corporations and public private partnerships to redress the growing disparity between developing and stagnating areas. Post modern design chaos and pollution tend to defeat the planning system. Decentralisation of powers for planning decisions create difficulties for professional planners as local culture relies on nepotism. Disparate planning powers need to converege into a more flexible mainstream system.

Read on: www.mpb.go.kr , http://gses.snu.ac.kr , www.kia.or.kr

93

PHILLIPPINES

FAST FACTS

- **Total Area:** 300,000 km²
- **Total Population:** 92,681,453
- **Population Growth:** 1.728%
- **Unemployment Rate:** 7.3%
- **GDP:** $298.9 billion
- **GDP per capita:** $3,300
- **GDP growth rate:** 7.3%

SETTLEMENTS STRUCTURE

- **Capital City:** Manila
  1,581,082 pop

- **Largest City:** Quezon City
  2,173,831 pop

- **Density:** 309 pop/km²

- **Urban Population:** 63%

Political and administrative organisation
Republic composed of 3 island groups, 17 regions, 81 provinces, 131 cities and 41,995 barangays.

Administrative competence for planning
The National Land Use Committee is responsible for the preparation of an integrated national physical framework plan. The Ministry of Housing and Urban Development Coordinating Council ratifies the comprehensive land use plans and zoning ordinances. The provincial and regional land use committees prepare physical framework plans. The Development Councils of the provinces, cities and municipalities prepare socio-economic plans. Since devolution in 1991 more responsibilities are vested in local government. The Barangay Development Council prepares land use plans.

Main planning legislation
Statutory provisions were provided for the establishment of a national building code (1977), an environmental code (1977), preparation of comprehensive land use plans (1993), the preparation of town plans (1991), the protection of designated areas (1992), and the preparation of comprehensive land use plans (1993). The Local Government Code sets out the plan making powers of the provincial, city, municipal and barangay councils.

Planning and implementation instruments
The national framework for physical planning 2002-2030 formulates policies for settlements, the use and protection of agricultural land, and the provision of infrastructure. The equivalent regional physical framework plan makes provision for the distribution of population, access to economic opportunities and social services, investment and environmental protection. The comprehensive land use plans prepared by the cities and municipalities articulate the spatial elements of the national and regional plans.

Development control
The Housing and Land Use Regulatory Board handles development control policies and compliance.

Planning system in practice
The planning system is well established in theory with enforcement procedures in place. However, cultural differences, i.e. languages, impede on the effectiveness of the planning process. Migration is straining cities in dealing with the poor and unskilled population in informal settlements on the city fringes and on roofs in the city centres. Rigid plans based on unrealistic trend extrapolation and lacking monitoring and sanctioning mechanisms cannot cater for basic infrastructure and dynamic real world needs. NGOs are expected to step into a basically laissez faire situation with foreign aid. Polarisation is widening between the many urban poor in shanty towns and gated communities.

Read on: www.hudcc.gov.ph , www.neda.gov.ph , www.up.edu.ph , http://piep.org.ph/profile.html

SINGAPORE

FAST FACTS

- **Total Area:** 692.7 km²
- **Total Population:** 4,608,167
- **Population Growth:** 1.135%
- **Unemployment Rate:** 1.7%
- **GDP:** $222.7 billion
- **GDP per capita:** $48,900
- **GDP growth rate:** 7.5%

SETTLEMENTS STRUCTURE

- **Capital City:** Singapore
  3,438,600 pop
- **Second City:** -
- **Density:** 6,652 pop/km²
- **Urban Population:** 100%

Political and administrative organisation
Republic composed of 5 regions and a number of urban districts.

Administrative competence for planning
The government is responsible for the definition and implementation of the land use planning system. The Cabinet takes the lead in coordinating research, and evaluating the requests from all the ministries. This information is forwarded to the Urban Development Authority which is responsible for the preparation of land use plans. These plans require the final approval by the Cabinet.

Main planning legislation
The government has passed a series of Acts which address the problems of land ownership, compulsory purchase, the assessment of compensation, and the resettlement rates for those firms and persons who are forced to relocate their premises and homes. Any increase in the value of land which results from the development plan proposals is shared between the government and the landowner.

Planning and implementation instruments
The 2002 concept plan, which defines the country's urban structure, is the key reference document with regard to the development and use of land. Its provisions are subject to minor review every 5 years and to major review every 20 years. Some 55 development guide plans have been prepared for urban districts that are relatively self-sufficient. Particular importance is attached to the identification of rigorous quantified environmental planning performance standards.

Development control
A complex system has been set up for the exercise of public control over the development and use of land. The Building and Construction Authority prepares and approves the building plans. The provisions of these plans are enforced by the Urban Redevelopment Authority which is responsible for granting permission for development proposals.

Planning system in practice
Importance is attached to the identification and safeguarding of sites for future iconic projects. Centrally planned and controlled, Singapore has been successful in providing spaces for its rapidly expanding and competitive economy. The need for structural economic change will affect also the planning system which has to accommodate both more diversity and diversification led by the market and changing demands. The strategy to attract advanced economic sectors and their highly mobile international personnel demands a more flexible approach. However, the trend is to support real estate development as a highly profitable commodity sector, rather than a tool of longer term sustainable structural change which is particularly important in Singapore as it cannot expand territorially beyond its island limits.

Read on: www.mnd.gov.sg , www.rst.nus.edu.sg , www.sip.org.sg

FAST FACTS

- **Total Area:** 35,980 km²
- **Total Population:** 22,920,946
- **Population Growth:** 0.238%
- **Unemployment Rate:** 3.9%
- **GDP:** $690.1 billion
- **GDP per capita:** $29,800
- **GDP growth rate:** 5.5%

SETTLEMENTS STRUCTURE

- **Capital City:** Taipei
  2,722,600 pop
  7,871,900 (metro. area)
- **Second City:** Kaohsiung
  1,514,900 pop
- **Density:** 640 pop/km²
- **Urban Population:** 81%

Political and administrative organisation

Multiparty democracy composed of 18 counties, 5 municipalities, and 2 special municipalities (Taipei and Kaohsiung).

Administrative competence for planning

The planning system is still very centralised. Government ministries are responsible for national physical and economic planning. The Construction and Planning Agency, in the Ministry of the Interior, is responsible for regional and local planning. The Ministry is also responsible for approving the master plans prepared by the planning districts. The Council for Economic Planning and Development approves the investment plans of public and private agencies.

Main planning legislation

The current legislation, which makes provision for regional and urban planning, incorporates many of the measures that were first adopted in 1964. The current land use planning system is district area based.

Planning and implementation instruments

There is a hierarchy of national, regional and local plans and plan implementation instruments. The national development plan 2002-7 formulates policies for: decentralisation of political power, public-private infrastructure partnerships, social cohesion, economic competitiveness and sustainability. There is a two-tier system of local plans. The city and district master plans provide a long-term comprehensive framework for development, and also designate the areas which require detailed planning. The detailed plans for these areas provide site specific guidance for the development and use of the land in question.

Development control

The district councils are responsible for exercising planning control over development proposals. They are empowered to issue building permits for development which complies with the land use and density provisions in the relevant local plans.

Planning system in practice

There is growing recognition of the need for the planning system to be more flexible in its response to changing political, economic and social circumstances while the juridical system remains refractory to change. Planning managed to achieve flexibility zoning in a special district plan which can accommodate activities in a less rigid way by balancing interests of land owners, the public sector and the market. Its triple helix concept combines innovative industrial production with living accommodation and environmental ecology on the same site at a pace which follows demand. Expropriation measures have assisted this change in urban development planning to make land available when it is required but without developing inappropriate premises and infrastructure. Greater public participation is needed to achieve combined competitiveness and social cohesion .

Read on: www.moi.gov.tw; www.up.fcu.edu.tw; www.capmi.gov.tw

VIETNAM ★

FAST FACTS

- **Total Area:** 329,560 km²
- **Total Population:** 86,116,559
- **Population Growth:** 0.99%
- **Unemployment Rate:** 5.1%
- **GDP:** $222.5 billion
- **GDP per capita:** $2,600
- **GDP growth rate:** 8.5%

SETTLEMENTS STRUCTURE

- **Capital City:** Hanoi
  1,396,500 pop
  2,543,700 (metro. area)
- **Second City:** Ho Shi Minh
  3,415,300 pop
- **Density:** 261 pop/km²
- **Urban Population:** 27%

Political and administrative organisation
Republic composed of 59 provinces, 5 metropolitan cities, urban and rural districts, and communes.

Administrative competence for planning
The Ministries of Natural Resources and Environment, Construction, Planning and Investment are responsible for land use change, spatial planning, and settlement planning and investment. Other ministries have a land use coordinating role with respect to agriculture, industry, transportation, health, education and sport.

Main planning legislation
Although the Land Law 1993 confirms that the state owns all the land, provision is made for the delegation of use, rent and transfer rights. The Construction Law 2003 makes provision for the preparation of regional, urban and rural land use plans.

Planning and implementation instruments
The plans prepared by the ministries constitute the legal basis for any development undertaken by the Ministry of Construction. The spatial regional, urban and rural construction plans make provision for the future development of designated areas, settlements and infrastructure. These plans are prepared and approved by the appropriate level of government; once approved they constitute the construction guidelines which have to be complied with. Major development proposals are submitted to the Prime Minister for approval.

Development control
The Construction Law sets out strong sanctions to ensure that the development and use of land complies with the planning guidelines. Developers have to obtain planning and investment licences and a land certificate before they can proceed.

Planning system in practice
Although there is still a strong emphasis on state involvement in spatial planning, current development pressures require an even greater planning effort than under the planned economy. Resisting market pressures with outdated regulatory planning mechanism act against the development potential of the country and efforts are being made to delegate some planning powers, responsibilities and initiatives to local authorities. Both land owners and land users request appropriate development procedures including infrastructure provision for inward investment. Nevertheless, barriers remain. While land values are recognised the land market remains narrowly regulated which distorts the price mechanism and thwarts a proactive planning process. Stringent building regulations contradict the inappropriate planning procedures which are subjected to a strong hierarchy of decision making focused on plan making with many bureaucratic hurdles. In reality, developers tend to bypass plans with the result of de facto chaotic development.

Read on: www.mpi.gov.vn; www.hau.edu.vn; www.icmd-cidm.ca

AUSTRALIA

FAST FACTS

- **Total Area:** 7,686,850 km²
- **Total Population:** 20,600,856
- **Population Growth:** 0.8%
- **Unemployment Rate:** 4%
- **GDP:** $766.8 billion
- **GDP per capita:** $37,500
- **GDP growth rate:** 4%

SETTLEMENTS STRUCTURE

- **Capital City:** Canberra
  327,700 pop
- **Second City:** Sydney
  4,250,100 pop
- **Density:** 3 pop/km²
- **Urban Population:** 93%

Political and administrative organisation
Constitutional monarchy with a federal parliamentary democracy composed of 6 states, 2 territories and 673 councils.

Administrative competence for planning
The states and local governments are responsible for land use planning, the latter being relatively weak. The states can devise their own planning laws which may allocate planning powers to municipalities. The Commonwealth government can influence land use and environmental protection via international treaties and indirectly through federal legislation on housing tenure, transportation, and other aspects of physical development.

Main planning legislation
Planning law differs from state to state; e.g. Western Australia Town Planning and Development Act 1928. Each state has a planning law which determines competences for plan preparation and implementation, including development control and enforcement, allocated to government agencies or municipalities.

Planning and implementation instruments
There is no national plan. Planning strategies usually devised at state level can be stand alone documents or take the form of regulations or regional plans. Local plans, prepared by local authorities are not prescriptive and leave a lot of flexibility within decision criteria. They have to be approved at state level, although some states distinguish between statutory and voluntary arrangements. Most change is initiated by a specific sector while plans ensure sustainability, economic prosperity, social justice and cultural recognition.

Development control
Development is controlled at the local level according to state, regional and local criteria. Distinction is made between permitted development, land use change which requires a permit and prohibited developments and uses. Sectoral agencies are self regulated quasi planning authorities.

Planning system in practice
Albeit reactive, planning seems to be at the right level as it is not perceived as controversial, however it favours urban sprawl which is seen as environmentally damaging. There is no coordination at federal level despite spatial impacts of national resource allocations. Conversely, the local level lacks implementation powers. Environmental issues, including water shortage, greater spatial polarity of wealth and service access present new planning challenges and their resolution would require better vertical and horizontal coordination across a very large and unevenly populated country. Neo-liberalism undermined sectoral coordination and the elimination of the regional planning level in a number of states weakened vertical coordination. Planning remains reactive with limited responsibilities at local level which is mainly regulatory.

Read on: www.dpi.wa.gov.au ; www.planning.nsw.gov.au ; www.dipnr.nsw.gov.au; www.udia.com.au, www.lincoln.ac.nz/esdd; www.rmit.edu.au; www.abp.unimelb.edu.au; www.aius.org.au; www.une.edu.au

NEW ZEALAND

FAST FACTS

- **Total Area:** 268,680 km²
- **Total Population:** 4,173,460
- **Population Growth:** 0.97%
- **Unemployment Rate:** 3.5%
- **GDP:** $112.6 billion
- **GDP per capita:** $27,300
- **GDP growth rate:** 3%

SETTLEMENTS STRUCTURE

- **Capital City:** Wellington
  165,100 pop
- **Largest City:** Auckland
  359,500 pop
  369,300 (metro. area)
- **Density:** 15 pop/km²
- **Urban Population:** 86%

Political and administrative organisation
Constitutional monarchy with a parliamentary democracy 12 regions, 5 unitary councils, 15 cities and 57 districts.

Administrative competence for planning
Due to the importance of New Zealand's coast, the Minister of Conservation has responsibility for statutory planning of coast related issues. Regional councils are entrusted with regional strategic plans and environmental resource management. Local councils are responsible for local development plans, land use and subdivision, and development control and they have contributing powers in resource management and are the first instance to grant resource consent.

Main planning legislation
Legislation is effect based and promotes planning by issue. The key law is the Local Government CT 2002. Environmental and resource management are regulated by the Resource Management Act 1991 which replaced the 1974 Town and Country Planning Act and also regulates spatial planning, development and land use. New Zealand's history explains the emphasis on environmental resources. There is separate legislation for military, national parks and conservation and resource extraction. Monitoring of development effects is mandatory.

Planning and implementation instruments
The New Zealand Coastal Policy Statement is the only national policy statement. Regional councils may prepare regional policy statements and non statutory plans. They can also prepare annual plans and asset plans which form part of local authority planning instruments. Participation is related to direct involvement in project proposals.

Development control
Permitted, controlled and discretionary and prohibited activities are regulated and controlled at the local level based, if necessary, on Environmental Impact Assessments.

Planning system in practice
The planning system is entirely focused on resource management and subordinates land use to broader environmental conservation principles. This foresighted approach, developed from an original indigenous standpoint after decolonisation, may well be able to cope better than traditional land use planning systems with increasing demands on indigenous resources, as well as effects of climate change such a thinning of the ozone layer, already felt in New Zealand. An approach based on capacity assessment and management of resources and in particular of resource requirements for spatial development may also assist in future to cope with planning pressures owing to increased demand on land and land use, possibly by the increase of future in-migration trends.

Read on: www.mfe.govt.nz ; www.dbh.govt.nz; www.lgnz.co.nz;
www.creative.auckland.ac.nz; www.rmla.org.nz; www.nzplanning.co.nz;
www.nzarm.org.nz; www.rmla.org.nz/index.aspx

SAMOA

FAST FACTS

- **Total Area:** 2,944 km²
- **Total Population:** 217,083
- **Population Growth:** 1.322%
- **Unemployment Rate:** NA%
- **GDP:** $1.029 billion
- **GDP per capita:** $5,400
- **GDP growth rate:** 6%

SETTLEMENTS STRUCTURE

- **Capital City:** Apia
  37,237 pop
- **Second City:** Salelologa
  6,062 pop

- **Density:** 74 pop/km²
- **Urban Population:** 23%

Political and administrative organisation
Independent state composed of 11 districts. The central governance framework is administered by the central government whereas local village affairs are governed by the social network based on traditions and custom known as the 'fa'a matai' (chiefly norms).

Administrative competence for planning
The Planning and Urban Management Agency responsible for land use and development control is a division under the auspices of the Ministry of Natural Resources and Environment.

Main planning legislation
The Planning and Urban Management Act 2004 sets the institutional arrangements, responsibilities and accountabilities for the implementation of the planning legislation. Other regulations are Planning and Urban Management (Environmental Impact Assessment) Regulations 2007 and the Planning and Urban Management (Development Consent Application and Fees) Regulations 2008.

Planning and implementation instruments
The Agency may develop physical plans through the statutory process outlined in the PUMA. The Agency has a range of growth strategies to support the sustainable management of natural and physical resources of Samoa: the Coastal Infrastructure Management Strategy, the Coastal Infrastructure Management Plans, the Sustainable Management Plans, the Integrated Urban Planning and Management System and the Strategy for the Development of Samoa (SDS) 2008-2012.

Development control
The environmental impacts of activities are primarily controlled by the PUMA through the requirement to apply for development consents. The development consent provides permission to carry out an activity so long as it complies with any conditions attached to the consent.

Planning system in practice
The Samoan planning system came into practice in 2004 and its key feature is the introduction of the philosophy of sustainable and integrated management of resources. The Agency has effectively developed regulations and policies to assist in development control. It increasingly administers a significant amount of consent applications, responds to amenity complaints in a timely and professional manner, strengthened its referral procedures with relevant authorities, maintained the direction and involvement of the Planning and Urban Management Board, focused on staff skills development and increased awareness of general and specific activities under the PUMA. On the other hand, there is significantly more pressure for the Agency to increase awareness, outreach and information dissemination, improve the compliance and monitoring programme, increase resources to ensure improved operational efficiencies and effectiveness and to fine tune enforcement activities.

Read on: http://www.mnre.gov.ws

Europe

EUROPEAN UNION
Austria
Belgium
Bulgaria
Cyprus
Czech Republic
Denmark
Estonia
Finland
France
Germany
Greece
Hungary
Ireland
Italy
Latvia
Lithuania
Luxembourg
Malta
Netherlands
Poland
Portugal
Slovakia
Slovenia
Spain
Sweden
United Kingdom

EUROPEAN ECONOMIC AREA AND BILATERAL
Iceland
Norway
Switzerland

NON EUROPEAN UNION
Albania
Armenia
Azerbaijan
Bosnia
Croatia
Georgia
Kosovo
Macedonia
Russia
Serbia
Turkey

Europe

AUSTRIA

FAST FACTS

- **Total Area:** 83,870 km²
- **Total Population:** 8,205,533
- **Population Growth:** 0.064%
- **Unemployment Rate:** 4.3%
- **GDP:** $319.7 billion
- **GDP per capita:** $39,000
- **GDP growth rate:** 3.3%

SETTLEMENTS STRUCTURE

- **Capital City:** Vienna
  1,523,600 pop
  2,041,300 (metro area)
- **Second City:** Graz
  219,500 pop
- **Density:** 98 pop/km²
- **Urban Population:** 67%

Political and administrative organisation
Federal Republic consisting of 9 autonomous states and about 2,200 communities.

Administrative competence for planning
The role of the state is limited but for the growing importance of EU policies and structural funds. Nevertheless, there is no national plan. Individual federal ministries prepare sectoral plans, e.g. for energy, traffic, water and the protection of the environment. The nine states are responsible for state and regional planning legislation and operational planning, as well as for verifying the local plans prepared by the cities and municipalities. In some instances, municipalities form communities of interest for issues which cross their borders.

Main planning legislation
Each state has its own planning legislation and administrative procedures. However, in all states, the cities and municipalities are empowered to prepare local development strategies, land use plans and local development plans.

Planning and implementation instruments
The plans prepared by the states have only a limited impact. Spatial development strategies for specific areas, provinces or municipalities, are set out in provincial and municipal strategic plans and local development schemes by the respective autonomous authorities in question, whilst the land use plans make provision for the general zoning and use of land. The local development plans also provide detailed guidance for the development and use of land, and for the setting, height and bulk of buildings.

Development control
The provisions of the local development plans have to be observed by land owners and prospective developers. They have to apply for a building permit for any development which does not accord with these provisions.

Planning system in practice
A hierarchical approach to planning ensures that the plans prepared at the local level have regard to the provisions of the plans drawn up by the state and at regional levels which, in turn, do have regard to national policies and standards. Increased attention needs to be paid to the problems of urban sprawl and rural decline. Similarly, environmental issues such as CO_2 emissions are not closely related to spatial planning. Likewise, renewable energy policies need greater connection with physical planning for easier implementation. With the enlargement of the EU, especially Lower Austria has acquired new development potential. Setting up Centrope, an institution with formal political commitments by its regional members from four adjoining countries, including the two capitals of Austria and Slovakia, provides supra-national, strategic planning opportunities for large scale, cross border projects.

Read on: www.austria.gv.at; http://oerok.gv.at; www.corp.at; www.wu-wien.ac.at; www.oir.at; www.tuwien.ac.at

FAST FACTS

- **Total Area:** 30,528 km²
- **Total Population:** 10,403,951
- **Population Growth:** 0.106%
- **Unemployment Rate:** 7.6%
- **GDP:** $378.9 billion
- **GDP per capita:** $36,500
- **GDP growth rate:** 2.7%

SETTLEMENTS STRUCTURE

- **Capital City:** Brussels
  981,200 pop
  1,750,600 (metro area)
- **Second City:** Antwerp
  450,000 pop
- **Density:** 341 pop/km²
- **Urban Population:** 97%

Political and administrative organisation
Constitutional Monarchy composed of three main independent regions: Wallonia, the Flemish region and Brussels.

Administrative competence for planning
The federal level has no competence for spatial planning, the regions, provinces, districts and municipalities have planning powers based on the subsidiarity principle. They vary between the three regions but are mainly bottom up. There is little coordination between the regions, but there exists cross border cooperation at European level through the European Spatial Development Perspective (ESDP).

Main planning legislation
Since the reform of the 1980 constitution planning legislation is devolved to the regions, thus there is no unified planning legislation in Belgium as a whole. In the Flemish region the administrative level and the communities were merged, thus planning is more comprehensive than in the other regions where socio-economic goals are separated from physical planning. Brussels has special planning issues as the seat of European organisations.

Planning and implementation instruments
All regions are producing regional development perspectives and structure plans. In some regions there exist provincial plans, and in all regions municipalities draw up local development frameworks, land use plans and detail plans. The private sector has limited initiative powers. Environmental impacts form part of planning through the country.

Development control
Each planning level is responsible for its own plan making and approval, within the regional spatial development framework which includes socio-economic and environmental goals. Building permits are the responsibility of the municipality.

Planning system in practice
Flanders decided to simplify its planning system to make it more flexible and less redundant as regards external changes, especially at the lowest tier, where partial revisions can be undertaken. However lack of vertical coordination for such changes may hamper their implementation. Moreover, continuous revision may jeopardise the stability of the planning system. The regional plan for the autonomous Brussels region is very general and leaves spatial specifications to the lower tier which may weaken the coherence of spatial planning in the city. The new Walloon spatial framework prevents comprehensive reviews of lower tier plans and this may lead to incoherence of local spatial objectives although they have been simplified in the new planning procedures.

Read on: www.ruimtelijkeordening.be; http://mrw.wallonie.be/DGATLP; www.urbanistes.be; www.isuru.be

Political and administrative organisation
Republic composed of 28 provinces (oblast) and 264 municipalities.

Administrative competence for planning
The Council of Ministers is responsible for defining the guiding principles of spatial planning policy. These principles are elaborated by the Spatial Planning Department of the Ministry of Regional Development and Public Works. The District Governors are responsible for the implementation of the National Development Scheme. The municipalities implement spatial planning activities in their areas.

Main planning legislation
The Spatial Planning Act 2001 has set out the main principles which underpin the planning system. These include equality of property rights, the balance between public and private interests, the supremacy of public interest in respect of strategic development and the integration of spatial planning and regional development. The Regional Development Act 2004 spells out further detailed procedures, in particular in respect to public works. A number of separate acts regulate rural development including agriculture and forestry, and the scope and contents of public works and other investment projects. Several ordinances concern regional development and public development.

Planning and implementation instruments
The spatial development plans and schemes make provision for the harmonisation of spatial planning and economic development with environmental protection. There exist regional and district spatial development schemes. These are supported by municipal masterplans and detailed plans which provide for the development of individual sites, the provision of infrastructure and the rehabilitation of damaged areas, as well as the protection of cultural and historic heritage.

Development control
The District Directorates exercise control over the issue of building permits and ensure that proposed development observes the provisions of spatial plans and related legislation. Municipalities are vested with the control of compliance with their spatial development plans and building permits.

Planning system in practice
After abandonment of the communist planning system in the 1980s which was very centralised, the introduction of a decentralised planning system has highlighted the need for greater harmonisation of spatial and economic planning. To date, the regional development procedures make no provision for the integration of regional economic development and spatial planning. There is a move though to integrate the foreseen national spatial development strategy with regional spatial policies. Lack of resources has impeded detailed local planning. This may prevent local spatial development policies from being integrated at the regional level at the next round of plan revision. Local plans are also needed to implement the new legal status of property and land.

Read on: www.mrrb.government.bg; www.ncrdhp.bg; www.uacg.bg

FAST FACTS

- **Total Area:** 110,910 km²
- **Total Population:** 7,262,675
- **Population Growth:** -0.813%
- **Unemployment Rate:** 8%
- **GDP:** $86.73 billion
- **GDP per capita:** $11,800
- **GDP growth rate:** 6.1%

SETTLEMENTS STRUCTURE

- **Capital City:** Sofia
  1,088,700 pop
- **Second City:** Plovdiv
  338,200 pop
- **Density:** 65 pop/km²
- **Urban Population:** 71%

FAST FACTS

- **Total Area:** 9,250 km^2
- **Total Population:** 792,604
- **Population Growth:** 0.522%
- **Unemployment Rate:** 3.8%
- **GDP:** $21.41 billion
- **GDP per capita:** 27,100
- **GDP growth rate:** 4.4%

SETTLEMENTS STRUCTURE

- **Capital City:** Nicosia
  197,600 pop
- **Second City:** Limassol
  180,100 pop
- **Density:** 86 pop/km^2
- **Urban Population:** 70%

Political and administrative organisation
Republic composed of 6 districts, 2 sovereign bases and the UN Green Line which separates the Greek and Turkish districts and some 42 municipalities.

Administrative competence for planning
The Planning Bureau, an independent body which operates under the aegis of the Ministry of Finance, is responsible for economic and regional development policies. Responsibility for spatial planning and urban policy rests with the Ministry of the Interior. The Department of Town Planning and Housing is the national directorate responsible for the implementation of planning legislation and aspects of urban policy and spatial planning. Two types of municipalities are planning for urban and rural areas respectively.

Main planning legislation
The 1972 Town and Country Planning Law set out the legal framework for the preparation of plans, the involvement of the public in planning, and the exercise of control over development proposals. Only the larger municipalities have competence over planning and development control.

Planning and implementation instruments
The main planning instruments consist of an island plan for the regional distribution of resources and development opportunities, local plans for major urban areas and other areas subject to intensive development pressures, and area schemes for the detailed planning and development of smaller areas. The aim of the Association of Cyprus Municipalities established in 1981 is to increase autonomy of local government including setting planning standards and development control conditions.

Development control
The Department of Town Planning and Housing has set up a directorate which is responsible for supervising the exercise of planning control over development. The district authorities are responsible for enforcing the detailed provisions of development plans, and for the enforcement of planning control.

Planning system in practice
The main spatial planning problem of Cyprus is its physical division into two territories and the lack of coordination between their respective development strategies. Although EU membership of Cyprus in 2004 covers the whole island, it was not able to change the status quo regarding integrated spatial planning. The physical division of the capital adds to these difficulties, as it is not possible to plan its overall spatial development and expansion, nor to contain its unregulated and uneven sprawl. Moreover, the effects of forced migration from the occupied territories is adding to unregulated suburban sprawl. The need exists for an island plan to provide a framework for regional plans which will have to address the problems posed by regional disparities in respect of employment, infrastructure and services.

Read on: www.planning.gov.cy; www.eng.ucy.ac.cy/ARCH; www.architecture.org.cy

FAST FACTS

- **Total Area:** 78,866 km²
- **Total Population:** 10,220,911
- **Population Growth:** -0.082%
- **Unemployment Rate:** 6.6%
- **GDP:** $249.1 billion
- **GDP per capita:** $24,400
- **GDP growth rate:** 5.7%

SETTLEMENTS STRUCTURE

- **Capital City:** Prague
  1,169,800 pop
  1,378,700 (metro. area)
- **Second City:** Brno
  376,400 pop
- **Density:** 130 pop/km²
- **Urban Population:** 75%

Political and administrative organisation
Republic composed of 14 regions, one of them the Capital City of Prague. Over 6200 municipalities, 13 with special status. 390 municipalities enjoy transfer of powers from the central government.

Administrative competence for planning
The Ministry for Regional Development is responsible for national planning. The regions, municipalities and communities are responsible for planning in their respective spatial jurisdictions. Plan preparation is outsourced to private individuals who have been approved by the Chamber of Architects.

Main planning legislation
Comprehensive planning was established with the 1948 planning and building act. The Planning and Building Act 1976, as amended, defines the activities, participants, documentation, procedures and mandatory aspects of land use planning. There is no legal requirement to prepare either a regional or a local plan. Other legislation on conservation, agriculture, forestry, and environmental impact assessment extends the influence of planning control. Other relevant legislation includes the Environmental Conservation Act, the Act and Decree on EIA, the Community Act, Road Act and Monument Conservation Law, the Agricultural Land Protection Act and Forest Law.

Planning and implementation instruments
The Planning and Building Act amended in 2000, determines a wide range of statutory planning instruments, including analytical spatial studies, regional, local and zoning plans, the designation of plot sub-division areas, and the designation of areas for special protection. The planning system is hierarchical and takes notice of European spatial policies. In particular, polycentric settlement development policies have repercussion on regional planning. Plans and planning regulations are statutory instruments and need approval by the planning tier above.

Development control
Permission has to be obtained from the Building Offices for a wide range of activities and changes of use. Failure to obtain permission can result in either the demolition of the building or the imposition of a fine, but is at the discretion of the Building Office.

Planning system in practice
After the demise of communism, planning was in disrepute. However, recent development pressures have highlighted the need to strengthen and reform the present planning system. The new Planning and Building Bill will make provision for the preparation, and bi-annual review of national and regional plans. Great distinctions were introduced between public and private property development, the latter benefiting from wide ranging flexibility. This means that planning has little control over private development proposals. The adoption of the guidelines of the European Spatial Development Perspective provided the need to reinstate regional planning and socio-economic programming.

Read on: http://old.mmr.cz; www.env.cz; www.fa.vutbr.cz; www.urbanismus.cz;

DENMARK

FAST FACTS

- **Total Area:** 43,094 km²
- **Total Population:** 5,484,723
- **Population Growth:** 0.295 %
- **Unemployment Rate:** 2,8 %
- **GDP:** $203.7 billion
- **GDP per capita:** $37,400
- **GDP growth rate:** 1.8%

SETTLEMENTS STRUCTURE

- **Capital City:** Copenhagen
  1,094,400 pop
- **Second City:** Århus
  220,700 pop
- **Density:** 127 pop/km²
- **Urban Population:** 86%

Political and administrative organisation
Constitutional monarchy composed of 5 regions and 98 municipalities.

Administrative competence for planning
The subsidiarity principle devolves planning and fiscal responsibilities to regional and local municipalities. The state remains responsible for the national planning framework and laying down the statutory content of plans. Planning competence of local authorities is to draw up vertically consistent frameworks for spatial development and management, comprehensive municipal plans, detailed local plans, control of development and land use.

Main planning legislation
The Planning Act of Denmark 2005 is ensuing local government reform and overhauling the 1970s legislation. It shifted from equal and balanced development to diverse and pluralistic spatial strategies, but providing equitable access to services for all citizens and more stringent environmental controls.

Planning and implementation instruments
The state issues national planning policies influenced by the European Spatial Development Perspective, directives, binding instructions and guidelines for regional and municipal planning and the environment. Regional development strategies and 12 year plans include business and environmental development objectives. Municipal plans and regulations include resource allocation, economic objectives, physical structure and land use and local plans for the whole area. All plans are revised after each election. Fully compensated expropriation is possible but not for land use allocation. Overall, planning was able to halt urban sprawl.

Development control
Development control is carried out by the authorities that devised the plans which are statutory.

Planning system in practice
Planning is equally concerned with spatial physical development and the preservation of the natural environment. Planning still aims to balance private property and property rights which are protected in the constitution with the common good, including what is embedded in the national heritage of buildings and wildlife. One success of the planning system is to have been able to curb second home sprawl and protect natural sites, and in particular the coast. Planning has been less successful in fostering functional and liveable cities. This efforts were undertaken to curb traffic congestion and social spatial segregation. They were redressed by a new urban regeneration policy based on public participation While successful in achieving compliance with plans the planning system cannot make developments happen. One of the finest aspects of Danish planning and regulations is that the system has been founded on dialogue and a "bottom up" perspective.

Read on: www.mim.dk/eng; www.fabnet.dk; www.plan.aau.dk; http://en.aarch.dk

FAST FACTS

- **Total Area:** 45,226 km²
- **Total Population:** 1,307,605
- **Population Growth:** -0.632%
- **Unemployment Rate:** 5.2%
- **GDP:** $29.35 billion
- **GDP per capita:** $21,800
- **GDP growth rate:** 7.3%

SETTLEMENTS STRUCTURE

- **Capital City:** Tallinn
  379,000 pop
- **Second City:** Tartu
  100,100 pop
- **Density:** 29 pop/km²
- **Urban Population:** 70%

Political and administrative organisation
Republic composed of 15 counties which are divided into 34 urban and 6193 rural districts.

Administrative competence for planning
The Ministry of Internal Affairs is responsible for planning; the Ministry of Economy and Communication is responsible for building control, and the Ministry of Culture is responsible for architectural and design advice. Although there is no formal second level of self-government, county government and municipalities are carrying out comprehensive and detail planning. They are expected to secure their implementation as well as public participation.

Main planning legislation
The Planning and Building Acts 2003 define the statutory planning system and make provision for the exercise of control over building activities, replacing the 1995 Act which was put into place after independence. Further supplements are being prepared.

Planning and implementation instruments
The National Planning Policy Statement formulates a strategy for the long-term sustainable development of the country. The county plans develop this strategy with respect to the conservation of agricultural land and natural resources, landscape protection, transportation and public utilities. Every rural municipality has to prepare a Comprehensive Plan which defines urban and rural areas, establishes the general conditions for the use of land and water, and provides for the conservation of historic and natural heritage. Detailed plans deal with plot-subdivision, building bulk, the space between buildings, easements and design requirements. The private sector can initiate development plans.

Development control
Permission is required for the construction of new buildings and the extension of existing buildings. The local councils can grant permission for changes of use, but they are not involved in the ratification of, and compliance with the planning system.

Planning system in practice
The present division of responsibility for planning, building control and architectural design is presenting difficulties. Unfortunately, in the latest reform, the ministry of the environment was omitted from the planning process, despite other policies which subscribe to sustainable development elsewhere. While the new planning system is based on legislation of Finland and Sweden, Estonia has still to undertake property reform with the aim to reinstate property rights of previous owners before expropriation in 1940 with the goal to reach the pre-war situation. The liberal approach to property ownership tends to contradict the legislation based on a more communally based Scandinavian approach and presents difficulties in applying planning legislation in practice.

Read on: www.envir.ee; www.emu.ee; www.planeerijad.ee

FINLAND ✚

FAST FACTS

- **Total Area:** 338,145 km²
- **Total Population:** 5,244,749
- **Population Growth:** 0.112%
- **Unemployment Rate:** 6.9%
- **GDP:** $185.9 billion
- **GDP per capita:** $35,500
- **GDP growth rate:** 4.4%

SETTLEMENTS STRUCTURE

- **Capital City:** Helsinki
  582,600 pop
  1,162,900 (metro. area)
- **Second City:** Espoo
  229,500 pop
- **Density:** 16 pop/km²
- **Urban Population:** 61%

Political and administrative organisation

Republic composed of 6 provinces, 19 regional councils and 432 municipalities. To facilitate co-operation and co-ordination the municipalities are grouped into 20 administrative regions and 74 sub-regions.

Administrative competence for planning

The land use department of the Ministry of Environment is responsible for planning legislation, national land use guidelines, environmental protection and land management. The state is also responsible for regional planning. Municipalities are in charge of local planning and development control. The state has operative offices at the municipal level. Local self governing municipalities with a strong tradition of independence can form associations to tackle common planning issues.

Main planning legislation

The Land Use and Building Act 2000 defines the law in respect of land use planning and building operations. Its provisions are supplemented by Acts governing nature conservation, the protection of buildings, natural resources, the prevention of environmental deterioration, and environmental impact assessment.

Planning and implementation instruments

Central government issues national land use policy guidelines which are then defined spatially in the plans prepared by the regional councils. These in turn are translated into site specific proposals in the local master plans and local detailed plans prepared by the municipalities.

Development control

The planning and building legislation includes certain general minimum requirements governing the granting of a building permit. In addition the local master plans set out specific criteria which have to be observed by prospective developers.

Planning system in practice

Because of the sparse population, land use has been based essentially on the principle that anybody can build anywhere for her/his own purpose. That spirit is still recognisable in the land use and planning legislation and in the building permits in rural areas. Late and rapid urbanisation has brought about dispersal and the most difficult planning problem today is urban sprawl and the spreading settlement structures. This also leads to unequal service and infrastructure provision which is not acceptable politically. The present planning system is deemed to be working quite well, despite the division of urban areas into independent and competing municipalities. Regional planning would need to be strengthened to improve coordination and generate more equitable spatial development. Public participation in planning is increasing due to greater interest by the public. However, the development industry is considering that it delays the planning process unduly. The same is considered of the complex appeal system in administrative courts and appeals to the supreme court are expected to be restricted in future.

Read on: www.environment.fi; www.maanmittauslaitos.fi; www.tkk.fi; www.tut.fi; www.sfhp.fi

FRANCE ▮▮

FAST FACTS

- **Total Area:** 547,030 km²
- **Total Population:** 60,876,136
- **Population Growth:** 0.574%
- **Unemployment Rate:** 8%
- **GDP:** $2.067 trillion
- **GDP per capita:** $33,800
- **GDP growth rate:** 1.8%

SETTLEMENTS STRUCTURE

- **Capital City:** Paris
  2,110,400 pop
  9,854,000 (metro. area)
- **Second City:** Marseille
  820,700 pop
- **Density:** 111 pop/km²
- **Urban Population:** 77%

Political and administrative organisation
Republic composed of 26 regions (4 overseas), 100 departments (4 overseas) and 36,678 municipalities (114 overseas).

Administrative competence for planning
France is the cradle of the nation state and state representation at lower tier levels through prefects. After decentralisation, the state is responsible for planning legislation, public utilities and guidance for lower tier planning. The directly elected regions are responsible for parks, inter-communal structures and spatial frameworks. Counties are in charge of sectoral coordination while the communes are sole competent for statutory land use planning and development control.

Main planning legislation
Land use plans were introduced in 1943. The code of planning lays down rights related to land. Legislation for development is contained in different acts. The Land Use Law 1967 generalised spatial planning. The Solidarity and Urban Renewal Law 2000 introduced sustainable development plans; the Planning and Housing Law 2002.

Planning and implementation instruments
Each administrative level produces its own plans. France also takes into account the European Spatial Development Perspective. Sectoctal plans for water, management, etc are the responsibility of the state. The newly introduced non standardised strategic plans at a regional level provide the framework for inter-communal and sustainable development consisting of a report, projects and implementation procedures. The local land use plans are more prescriptive and binding with detailed regulations, local public utilities, and distinction between developed, developable, agricultural and natural land. New sustainable development plans were introduced. Planning follows project management principles and has to allow for public participation. Local planning has been changed into a new local plan which contains general principles for spatial development, a land use plan, zoning and detail plan and land reserves for public infrastructure.

Development control
Communes are sole responsible for setting planning rules and building regulations and enforcing them.

Planning system in practice
The new spatial plans for sustainable development with clearly defined objectives for all planning and implementation levels with justifications but freely translated into space have changed the traditional French legalistic approach to planning. The private sector, as well as professionals are more involved. An increasing diversity of institutions has made small communes more operational in carrying out common urban projects. However inviolable property rights are hampering large scale integrated development strategies, especially when land owners are hoarding developable land. Also state budgeting for public utilities contradicts local development strategies.

Read on: www.plan.gouv.fr; www.certu.fr; www.diact.gouv.fr; www.urbanistes.com; http://aperau.org; www.iaurif.org; http://cfdu.free.fr; www.fnau.org:

FAST FACTS

- **Total Area:** 357,021 km²
- **Total Population:** 82,369,548
- **Population Growth:** -0.044%
- **Unemployment Rate:** 9.1%
- **GDP:** $2.833 trillion
- **GDP per capita:** $34,400
- **GDP growth rate:** 2.6%

SETTLEMENTS STRUCTURE

- **Capital City:** Berlin
  3,274,500 pop
  3,933,300 (metro. area)
- **Second City:** Hamburg
  1,686,100 pop
- **Density:** 231 pop/km²
- **Urban Population:** 89%

Political and administrative organisation

Federal Republic composed of 16 states which are divided into cities and counties, as well as municipalities.

Administrative competence for planning

The hierarchical allocation of planning powers between the federation and the states and the municipalities observes the principle of subsidiarity. Each planning decision is taken at the lowest possible political level. The Federal level has no direct planning competences, it only establishes frameworks which take account of other federal policies. The municipalities are the most sovereign bodies in the planning process, but they have to follow the principles and guidelines set out by higher tiers of planning. The states devise their own planning laws, and the regions are responsible for development strategies of their jurisdictions. Another planning principle is mutual influence which means that the states have to take into account local planning strategies when devising their plans, especially as regards infrastructure. Each planning level is responsible for specific planning tasks. which differ between the planning levels.

Main planning legislation

The federation has passed a Framework Act on Spatial Planning which sets out the regulations for municipal planning. Each state enacts its own legislation to regulate state and regional planning.

Planning and implementation instruments

The Federal government prepares a comprehensive framework for the spatial development of the whole country. Each state prepares its own spatial development plan, design guidance and building codes. The municipalities prepare both preparatory and legally binding land use plans. These plans define land use zones, density and building bulk.

Development control

The municipalities are responsible for development control within their jurisdictions. They are empowered to issue building permits for development proposals which observe the provisions of the detailed land use plans.

Planning system in practice

The planning system is having to adjust to rapidly changing circumstances since German Reunification. For example it has to become much more problem orientated. The need exists for new planning methods and processes. To fulfil the gap between formal planning and the needs of spatial development both at the local and super-local levels, informal planning processes are developed and implemented. Such informal planning processes attempt to reach consent and cooperation among the concerned actors in a planning matter in different ways. The integration of the European Union, trying to accelerate the establishment of the internal market, link peripheral regions to Europe and open itself to neighbouring countries, adds an additional planning level for the promotion of trans-European infrastructure-corridors.

Read on: www.bbr.bund.de; www.bmvbs.de; www.irb.fraunhofer.de; www.ioer.de;
www.bauhaus-dessau.de; www.isr.tu-berlin.de

FAST FACTS

- **Total Area:** 131,940 km²
- **Total Population:** 10,722,816
- **Population Growth:** 0.146%
- **Unemployment Rate:** 8.4%
- **GDP:** $326.4 billion
- **GDP per capita:** $30,500
- **GDP growth rate:** 3.7%

SETTLEMENTS STRUCTURE

- **Capital City:** Athens
  747,300 pop
  3,247,000 (metro area)
- **Second City:** Thessalonica
  361,200 pop
- **Density:** 81 pop/km²
- **Urban Population:** 61%

Political and administrative organisation
Republic composed of 15 regions, 54 districts, 900 municipalities and 133 communes.

Administrative competence for planning
The Ministry of Environment, Spatial Planning and Public Works is responsible for the preparation of national spatial development policies. As appropriate, other ministries contribute specialist inputs to the planning process. Each region prepares material for inclusion in the national development plan. The districts are responsible for local planning.

Main planning legislation
Greek planning legislation is based on the French system. The Spatial Planning Law 1999 sets out the legal framework for both national and regional planning. The Sustainable Urban Development Law 1997 defines the regulations and procedures for local planning. Building regulations and codes are set out in the 1985 Act which was last amended in 2000.

Planning and implementation instruments
There exists a hierarchical series of plans which operate at national, regional and local levels. The state elaborates the national territorial plan. It is also in charge of the special (sectoral) territorial plans which provide the framework for the operation and management of the planning system. It directs master plans and environmental protection programmes and ratifies plans of all planning levels. It also draws up regional plans. The regional territorial plans, special spatial plans and regulatory plans make provision for regional spatial planning, the protection of special areas and provide guidelines for urban plan preparation. The municipalities produce and are charged with the implementation of general urban plans. The planning system is top down.

Development control
The regulatory plans, which cover only 5 to 10% of the country, confirm the development rights of landowners. It is possible for landowners to undertake development outside the area of regulatory plans on plots with road access and of a specified minimum size. This leads to much illegal development and large scale urban sprawl.

Planning system in practice
The planning system remains centralised despite administrative decentralisaton during the 1980s and 1990s. Having focussed mainly on physical planning problems and issues, the new framework now attaches importance to strategic spatial planning. Regulatory plans are numerous and detailed, however only 5 to10% of the national territory is covered by regulatory plans. The gap between plans and reality is demonstrated by the unauthorised developments - one of the major challenges of the planning system. The same gap between regulatory instruments and reality exists in the field of environmental protection. While planning was focusing of controls within urbanised land, the new planning framework attempts to institute more strategic spatial planning, but no provisions are foreseen for better implementation and controls .

Read on: www.minenv.gr; www.sepox.gr; www.plandevel.auth.gr; www.upatras.gr; www.uth.gr; www.doxiadis.org

FAST FACTS

- **Total Area:** 93,030 km²
- **Total Population:** 9,930,915
- **Population Growth:** -0.254%
- **Unemployment Rate:** 7.1%
- **GDP:** $194.2 billion
- **GDP per capita:** $19,500
- **GDP growth rate:** 2.1%

SETTLEMENTS STRUCTURE

- **Capital City:** Budapest
  1,769,500 pop
  2,597,000 (metro. area)
- **Second City:** Debrecen
  210,500 pop
- **Density:** 107 pop/km²
- **Urban Population:** 66%

Political and administrative organisation
Republic composed of 19 counties and 3,156 municipalities.

Administrative competence for planning
The government is responsible for the definition of the planning system and building code. These provisions have to be observed by the municipalities, property owners and developers. All municipalities have wide discretionary powers. Planning decisions can only be annulled when contravening the law. The County Administration Offices and Special Purpose Agencies exercise legal control over local plans. Hungary is deeply embedded in codified law and final court decisions. Building Authorities are enforcing planning decisions in cities and larger town in rural areas.

Main planning legislation
The new Urban Planning Act 1997 on the Formation and Protection of the Built Environment, was adopted after seven years of preparatory work. The Act - modelled on German planning legislation - defines the statutory planning system, planning instruments and Building Codes. It also introduced four new planning tools: urban development concepts, structure plans, regulatory plans and local building codes. Very few planning standards are defined at the national level. Only the latter two are legally binding.

Planning and implementation instruments
The 1997 Act introduced the urban development concept, the structure plan, the regulatory plan and the local building code. The first two have to be observed by all local decision makers whereas the last two have to be strictly observed by property owners and developers. All agencies have to strictly observe the legal requirements set out in the statutes. Zoning and planning permissions which are closely linked to building permits which are aimed at the private sector as private initiatives are needed to implement the various plans.

Development control
Building authorities can issue a range of building permissions, including permissions to demolish buildings, for land sub-division and changes of use. Conditions can, and are, attached to these permissions. Enforcement procedures also exist and are often used.

Planning system in practice
The new Hungarian planning system is a mixture of different planning approaches (American, British, French and German) but the implementation of the proposed planning instruments and development controls have several difficulties in practice. An attempt has been made to strengthen the legal position of urban planning to prevent unwanted development. Procedures have been introduced to regularise illegal developments. This includes the provision that those who infringe the planning regulations have to pay fines. As the Building Authorities have some discretion over such decisions and such an arbitrary situation may lead to further infringements.

Read on: www.vati.hu; www.fvm.hu; www.kvvm.hu; www.mut.hu; www.ktk-ces.hu; www.rkk.hu; www.mri.hu

FAST FACTS

- **Total Area:** 70,280 km²
- **Total Population:** 4,156,119
- **Population Growth:** 1.133%
- **Unemployment Rate:** 5%
- **GDP:** $187.5 billion
- **GDP per capita:** $45,600
- **GDP growth rate:** 5.3%

SETTLEMENTS STRUCTURE

- **Capital City:** Dublin
  1,018,500 pop
- **Second City:** Cork
  193,400 pop
- **Density:** 59 pop/km²
- **Urban Population:** 60%

Political and administrative organisation
Republic composed of 6 regions and 26 county /city councils.

Administrative competence for planning
The Department of Environment, Heritage and Local Government prepares the national spatial strategy, having regard to the representations of some 17 government departments. The regional authorities prepare regional planning guidelines for their respective areas. The county/city councils are required to prepare and adopt development plans. The city or county manager has wide ranging effective executive powers including over planning matters, although the final say remains with the elected politicians.

Main planning legislation
The Planning and Development Act 2000 sets out the legislative framework for planning and sustainable development. It introduced a new hierarchy of plan, planning guidance and provision of affordable housing. The Local Government Act 2001 added further competences for lower government tiers, but the system remains centralised. The Planning and Development Regulations 2001 ensure more transparency of the planning system.

Planning and implementation instruments
The national planning strategy is a 20 year planning framework designed to achieve a better balance of social, economic and physical development. Each of the regional authorities is required to prepare and adopt regional plans as a long-term strategy for future development. The county/city councils are required to prepare statutory development plans. They are in charge of the operational level of the planning system, including development control. A system of incentives since 1986 are accelerating urban renewal initiatives. They include rural renewal schemes. Tax relief is also offered for the provision of public realm and open spaces.

Development control
The county/city councils are responsible for development control. Developers have to seek planning permission for all operations which fall within the legal definition of development. Provision is made for applications to be publicised and notice given to interested parties.

Planning system in practice
Despite the reform of the planning system economic growth continues to present challenges. Urban sprawl, affordable housing, rural housing and the implementation of strategic national policy are contentious issues. The pressure of the economic growth also pose challenges for the planning system itself and in some instances the implementation of the legislation has not had the desired effect. Development Corporations have been set up, for example in the Docklands of Dublin to accelerate the development process and effectively overrule the local planning powers. The National fflSpatial Strategy overrules all lower tier planning decisions and devises measures of international cooperation, especially with Northern Ireland. However, many challenges lay in the way of implementing the National Spatial Strategy despite its budgetary allocations.

Read on: www.environ.ie; www.enfo.ie; www.irishplanninginstitute.ie; www.ucd.ie

FAST FACTS

- **Total Area:** 301,230 km²
- **Total Population:** 58,145,321
- **Population Growth:** -0.019%
- **Unemployment Rate:** 6.7%
- **GDP:** $1.8 trillion
- **GDP per capita:** $31,000
- **GDP growth rate:** 1.9%

SETTLEMENTS STRUCTURE

- **Capital City:** Rome
  2,455,600 pop
  3,550,900 (metro area)
- **Second City:** Milan
  1,180,700 pop
- **Density:** 193 pop/km²
- **Urban Population:** 68%

Political and administrative organisation
Republic composed of 20 regions, instituted in 1971, five with special statutes, 103 provinces and 8,101 municipalities. The larger municipalities are subdivided into districts and neighbourhoods.

Administrative competence for planning
The state sets out the policies and regulations which constitute a framework for regional and urban planning. The regions are largely autonomous and can enact their own planning laws which must, however, take account of the national planning framework. Provinces draw up area plans and have some competences over municipalities. The municipal authorities are responsible for the preparation and adoption of detailed development plans and development control. Mountain communities are administering their areas, and parks have their own administrative entities.

Main planning legislation
The country has adopted a detailed complex planning system which is based on the National Urban Planning Law 1942. Subsequent legislation has broadened the scope of this system. The National and Regional Act is establishing the formal planning instruments. The Local Autonomy Code Law 1990 empowered the provinces to prepare provincial area plans. Some regions and municipal authorities have adopted their own laws which set out new zoning and environmental performance criteria. There is also the 2001 laws on large public works, and codes of cultural and landscape assets.

Planning and implementation instruments
Planning is hierarchic. The state establishes policies for regional and urban planning. The regions, provinces and municipal authorities have adopted instruments which reflect their respective levels of territorial jurisdiction. As appropriate they are also preparing structure plans, land use plans, master plans and action area plans. Special provisions exist for the protection of the environment, heritage and landscapes. Regions can also draw up plans which are not specifically mentioned in national legislation, such as coastal plans. Municipalities can draw up plans jointly with the private sector for specific areas.

Development control
The exercise of development control has been impeded by the Planning Amnesty laws. The law passed in 2004 has defined a range of illegal planning and building activities which can be given legal recognition.

Planning system in practice
Problems exist with respect to the participation of the public in the planning process. The detailed land use plans do not respond to the dynamic forces which give rise to development pressure. Nor do they make adequate provision for sustainable development. Urban sprawl remains uncontained and has an adverse effect on high quality landscapes. Under pressure of global competition cities tend to adopt icons which may not be compatible with the quality of traditional urban life.

Read on: www.apat.gov.it; www.minambiente.it; www.inu.it; www.urbanisti.it; www.diap.polimi.it; www.polito.it; www.architetturavallegiulia.it; www.unict.it

FAST FACTS

- **Total Area:** 64,589 km²
- **Total Population:** 2,245,423
- **Population Growth:** -0.629%
- **Unemployment Rate:** 5.9%
- **GDP:** $40.04 billion
- **GDP per capita:** $17,700
- **GDP growth rate:** 10.3%

SETTLEMENTS STRUCTURE

- **Capital City:** Riga
  706,200 pop
  867,700 (metro. area)
- **Second City:** Daugavpils
  111,700 pop
- **Density:** 35 pop/km²
- **Urban Population:** 66%

Political and administrative organisation

Republic composed of 5 regions, 26 districts, 7 cities with a separate status, 57 towns and 470 rural municipalities.

Administrative competence for planning

There is a hierarchical system in which the government is responsible for planning legislation and the formulation of a national planning framework. It also undertakes sectoral national planning. The regions, which have to observe this framework, prepare regional spatial plans, and the districts prepare detailed local land use plans and building codes. However, regional representatives are also participating in national plan formulation. Administrative territorial reform is continuing with the aim to form larger and stronger municipalities.

Main planning legislation

The Spatial Development Planning Law 1998 sets out the principles, objectives and tasks of planning. The Territorial Planning Law 2002 defines the planning system with its four levels, national, regional, district and local respectively, procedures and powers. Strategic development planning is likewise defined in the Regional Development Law 2002 which sets up five planning regions.

Planning and implementation instruments

The national plan sets out the broad planning framework which is then developed as appropriate in the regional, municipal and local detailed plans. The regional plans identify development potential, trends and requirements and assist with planning cooperation between municipalities. These in turn are further developed in the municipal and local detailed plans. The private sector is active in initiating plans.

Development control

The municipalities are responsible for development control and the issue of building permits for proposed building projects. Before issuing a permit recourse is made to the local detailed land use plans to ensure that the proposed development conforms with the planning criteria set out therein.

Planning system in practice

The planning system is still evolving reflecting the debate about the nature and purpose of planning. There is growing recognition of the need for a better understanding of urban decision-making systems. One of many serious drawbacks of the Latvian planning system is the lack of an enforced urban development strategy at the national level. The state impact on urban development matters is and will be rather limited and there are problems of integrated planning. The concept of urban planning is still an object of many discussions in Latvia were the total environment has changed radically over the last decade. The main planning problem at national level is the disbalance between the capital City of Riga and almost all the other Latvian territory and the lack of environmental protection. Planning education is being improved, together with decision making skills in the light of the complexity and dynamics of the cities and the demands of the sustainability agenda.

Read on: www.lv; www.lu.lv

FAST FACTS

- **Total Area:** 65,200 km²
- **Total Population:** 3,565,205
- **Population Growth:** -0.284%
- **Unemployment Rate:** 3.2%
- **GDP:** $59.59 billion
- **GDP per capita:** $16,700
- **GDP growth rate:** 8%

SETTLEMENTS STRUCTURE

- **Capital City:** Vilnius
  543,500 pop
- **Second City:** Kaunas
  379,800 pop
- **Density:** 55 pop/km²
- **Urban Population:** 66%

Political and administrative organisation
Republic composed of 10 counties and 60 municipalities.

Administrative competence for planning
A hierarchical system has been adopted whereby the government determines the legal framework and general guidelines for territorial planning, policy formulation and plan implementation. The regional plans apply national planning guidelines and provide a context for the preparation of municipal, district and local detailed plans drawn up by the municipalities. The regions are also in charge for drawing up county plans.

Main planning legislation
The Spatial Planning Law 1995 sets out the responsibilities and arrangements for planning in general and for land use control in particular, and sets out responsibility for controlling plan compliance. Supplementary rules and regulations have since been adopted by the government and the Ministry of the Environment.

Planning and implementation instruments
The National Plan adopted in 2002 defines the spatial strategy for the development and use of land. It also sets out the principles which must be observed to secure the preservation of the nation's cultural and environmental heritage. The regional plans identify current trends, development pressures and infrastructure needs. The district plans have to observe the provisions of the national plan and the relevant regional plan. They also regulate the location of high rise buildings and infrastructure development in special plans in order to protect the local cultural and natural heritage. The detailed local plans identify individual building sites and plots. They have statutory status and control all local construction and infrastructure works.

Development control
All prospective developers must seek the approval of the appropriate authority. Development proposals must observe the provisions of the relevant spatial and detail plans and their enforcement is the responsibility of municipalities. The courts are the last resort of planning appeals.

Planning system in practice
A hierarchical approach to planning ensures consistency. The new planning system is still evolving and has to cope with the problems and outcomes of rapid economic and social change following independence and membership of the European Union. In the light of the lack of infrastructure and the physical adjustments required to accommodate the new national socio-economic objectives the planning legislation and the administrative competences are under continuous revision. The first master plans have not been able to co-ordinate either public or private investment decisions. As a consequence there have been spontaneous "waves" of unregulated strategic planning initiatives. Although public participation in planning is very formal the role of the public is unclear and needs clarification. Increasing nimbyism is delaying the implementation of common interest and advice is sought for a more balanced participation system. However, there is a lack of professional planners and training provisions.

Read on: www.am.lt; www.lgt.lt; www.corpi.ku.lt; www.mab.lt

LUXEMBOURG ▬

FAST FACTS

- **Total Area:** 2,586 km²
- **Total Population:** 486,006
- **Population Growth:** 1.188%
- **Unemployment Rate:** 4.4%
- **GDP:** $38.79 billion
- **GDP per capita:** $80,800
- **GDP growth rate:** 5%

SETTLEMENTS STRUCTURE

- **Capital City:** Luxembourg
  78,800 pop
- **Second City:** Esch-Alzette
  24,255 pop
- **Density:** 188 pop/km²
- **Urban Population:** 92%

Political and administrative organisation
Constitutional monarchy composed of 3 regions, 12 cantons and 116 communes.

Administrative competence for planning
A two-tier system is in operation whereby the government is responsible for national spatial planning and the municipalities for local planning. The Ministry of the Interior and Spatial Planning co-ordinates the relevant European, national and local planning policies. The municipal authorities are responsible for town planning, local development, urban regeneration and development control. Planning follows the subsidiarity principle. Municipalities can cooperate and constitute regional syndicates for more efficient planning and implementation of infrastructure projects and urban service provision.

Main planning legislation
The planning system is defined in the 1999 Spatial Development Act. Its has been supplemented in 2004 by legislation which deals with city development and with the protection of natural resources and the environment.

Planning and implementation instruments
The National Spatial Planning Programme, which was revised in 2003, sets out the government's spatial objectives for sustainable development in a non-biding document. Further guidance is provided in the Integrated Transport and Spatial Development Concept of 2004, and in the Guiding Sectoral Plans. Regional plans are not legally binding. The land use plans and the legally binding development plans prepared by the municipal authorities provide detailed policies for the development and use of land. Luxembourg is participating in many cross-border spatial developments and EU spatial development programmes.

Development control
New instruments, such as the creation of a building obligation, the definition of development and the promotion of land mobilisation need to be introduced to facilitate development control.

Planning system in practice
Land use development and transportation planning is not integrated. The Government departments engaged in spatial, transportation and landscape planning need to improve co-operation and consultation, despite their declared policies of concentrated deconcentration and environmental protection.International commuting is putting a great strain on the infrastructure and the transportation system with congested roads and related pollution. This has brought about ribbon developments which the planning system seemed to be unable to contain. 'Rurbanisation' continues to erode the countryside and puts increasing demand on the road networks which is being continuously enlarged to the detriment of public transport. The one advantage of this otherwise negative spiral is that rural communities are obtaining new life as the urban population tends to settle there rather than in the suburb bu leads to relentless reduction of rural land.

Read on: www.gouvernement.lu/ministeres: www.snhbm.lu; www.uni.lu;
www.eukn.org/luxembourg

FAST FACTS

- **Total Area:** 316 km²
- **Total Population:** 403,532
- **Population Growth:** 0.407%
- **Unemployment Rate:** 6.3%
- **GDP:** $9.396 billion
- **GDP per capita:** $22,900
- **GDP growth rate:** 3.8%

SETTLEMENTS STRUCTURE

- **Capital City:** Valletta
  6,900 pop
  194,200 (metro area)
- **Second City:** Birkirkara
  21,600 pop
- **Density:** 1,277 pop/km²
- **Urban Population:** 92%

Political and administrative organisation
Republic composed of 68 local councils.

Administrative competence for planning
The Malta Environment and Planning Board (MEPA) is the main government body responsible for land use planning and environmental protection. It is accountable to the Malta Environment and Planning Authority under the Ministry for Rural Affairs and Environment. The MEPA Board provides strategic guidance for the three Development Control Commissions responsible for planning, environment protection and corporate services respectively. The Planning Directorate seeks to promote sustainable development through the preparation and implementation of development plans.

Main planning legislation
The Development Act 1992 made provision for the preparation of a structure plan for the Maltese Islands. It also established the Planning Appeals Boards to determine all planning appeals made by aggrieved persons.

Planning and implementation instruments
The MEPA Board provides strategic guidance for the Planning and the Environment Protection Directorates and ensures the legality of carrying out their responsibilities. The structure plan, together with various local plans, action plans, subject plans and development briefs constitute the framework for decisions in respect of the planning of the Maltese islands. The MEPA is in charge of preparing most of these plans. It has also issued planning guidance in respect of retail planning, design and fish farming. Government bodies, local councils, and private investors can all submit request for the promotion of change.

Development control
A number of bodies within the MEPA are empowered to approve applications for the development and use of land. There are three development control commissions, each in charge of different functional areas, vacant land, villa development, major projects including in unplanned areas, and conservation and rural areas.

Planning system in practice
There is still some scepticism about the need for, and role of planning. This, in part, reflects the lack of co-ordination between the various bodies involved in the determination of planning applications, and development control. The two appeals boards can overturn decisions and thereby compromise policies and plans and thus create inconsistencies which undermine the planning system. The enormous amount and rapid development along the coasts is eroding the landscape and the ecological balance of sensitive natural environments. While some historic sites and cultural heritage is protected many archaeological sites of international importance are under threat. However, pressures groups can be effective as they tend to have access to the influencial planning consultative committee and they have managed to preserve the minor island sfrom excessive development.

Read on: www.mepa.org.mt; www.um.edu.mt

FAST FACTS

- **Total Area:** 41,526 km²
- **Total Population:** 16,645,313
- **Population Growth:** 0.436%
- **Unemployment Rate:** 4.1%
- **GDP:** $638.9 billion
- **GDP per capita:** $38,600
- **GDP growth rate:** 3.5%

SETTLEMENTS STRUCTURE

- **Capital City:** Amsterdam
  751,757 pop
- **Second City:** Rotterdam
  584,046 pop
- **Density:** 401 pop/km²
- **Urban Population:** 67%

Political and administrative organisation
Constitutional monarchy composed of 12 provinces and 483 municipalities..

Administrative competence for planning
The state is responsible for enacting planning legislation and the preparation of national planning key-decisions document. The provincial governments are responsible the preparation of regional planning statements and general proposals for the development and use of land. The municipal authorities prepare the structure plans and detailed local land use plans.

Main planning legislation
The provisions of the Spatial Planning Act 1965, revised in 1985, are still valid today. The Act's provisions in respect of local projects were revised in 2000 to facilitate greater flexibility. Each administrative tier is free to determine its own planning goals and the content of its plans.

Planning and implementation instruments
The national planning key decisions document sets out the government's spatial policy aims, objectives and strategy. It also designates special areas such as nature reserves. The regional plans prepared by the provincial governments provide a framework for urban, industrial and recreational development. The municipal structure plans provide an area-wide framework for the future development of each area. The detailed and use plans prepared by the municipalities are legally enforceable.

Development control
The municipal authorities are responsible for development control and the issue of building permits. Permission is required for proposed land use changes and for the erection of buildings. Development proposals are required to conform to the provisions of the relevant land use plans.

Planning system in practice
Considering the existing planning process too slow, the new Spatial Planning Act - implemented in 2008 - contains new rules which focus on combining goals for an efficient and transparent policy development, substituting for the two pillar physical and environmental development strategies. It introduces objectives for a strict maintenance of law and order and simplified legal protection. Other important features are deregulation, decentralisation and a focus on development. The 2005 National Spatial Planning Strategy aims to strengthen international competitiveness, promoting strong cities and involving the state as an active partner in strategic infrastructure development projects, including in the Randstad, the largest Dutch conurbation. To that effect it has set up a new agency for national services and properties, and a separate agency for rural areas, together with a National Public Development Agency for complex regional developments. Modernisation of land policy aims at equitable cost and benefit distribution accrued by spatial developments. The new Land Development Act is supporting public private partnerships.

Read on: www.minvrom.nl; www.rivm.nl; www.ruimtelijkplanbureau.nl;

FAST FACTS

- **Total Area:** 312,685 km²
- **Total Population:** 38,500,696
- **Population Growth:** -0.045%
- **Unemployment Rate:** 12.8%
- **GDP:** $624.6 billion
- **GDP per capita:** $16,200
- **GDP growth rate:** 6.5%

SETTLEMENTS STRUCTURE

- **Capital City:** Warsaw
  1,607,600 pop
  2,201,900 (metro. area)
- **Second City:** Lodz
  778,200 pop
- **Density:** 123 pop/km²
- **Urban Population:** 62%

Political and administrative organisation
Republic composed of 16 provinces, 373 counties and 2,384 districts.

Administrative competence for planning
The government is responsible for national policy of physical development and for major planning decisions. The Department of Spatial Coordination is responsible for physical planning and land management. Other ministries are responsible for environmental and ecological policy, and for building code legislation. Provinces formulate regional development policy and coordinate public projects. The counties issue building permits and monitor building control. The districts prepare detailed local land use plans and are responsible for planning control.

Main planning legislation
The Spatial Planning and Spatial Development Act 2003 defines the basic goals and principles of spatial planning. Some planning standards and regulations are defined in the building code and Environmental Protection Act 2003. The Local Government Acts 1990 and 1998 lay down planning goals and procedures, together with the Public Administration Act 1998. The Real Estate Act 1997 lays down conditions and regulations for land division and expropriation.

Planning and implementation instruments
There exist four levels of planning. The government prepares statements of national development policy, goals, trends and the socio-economic assumptions which underpin policy. The provincial councils prepare regional physical development plans and coordinate public sector development programmes. The county councils prepare physical development studies and are responsible for the issue of building certificates. The districts prepare legally binding local physical development plans. At regional level, the representatives of the state and the head of the provincial government share different responsibilities.

Development control
The county levels are responsible for building control and the district councils are empowered to grant planning permission for development proposals within the provisions of the detailed local physical development plans.

Planning system in practice
The changes introduced in 2003 have not achieved expected results, in part, to the lack of a legal requirementto prepare local plans, thus impeding potential development and rehabilitation of areas. This constituted a serious barrier to new investment and the economic development of some regions. It has been also adverse to proper coordination of spatial development. A new planning bill intends to strengthen the planning and enforcement powers of the municipalities and to make the planning system sufficiently flexible to accommodate the current transformations of the economy and society. spatial planning in the city. It also accommodates more equitable compensation for land and real estate owners affected by planning strategies.

Read on: www.mos.gov.pl; www.sarp.org.pl; www.tup.org.pl; www.pg.gda.pl;

EUROPEAN UNION
PORTUGAL

FAST FACTS

- **Total Area:** 92,391 km²
- **Total Population:** 10,676,910
- **Population Growth:** 0.305%
- **Unemployment Rate:** 8%
- **GDP:** $232 billion
- **GDP per capita:** $21,800
- **GDP growth rate:** 1.9%

SETTLEMENTS STRUCTURE

- **Capital City:** Lisbon
  559,400 pop
  2,618,100 (metro area)
- **Second City:** Porto
  264,200 pop
- **Density:** 116 pop/km²
- **Urban Population:** 56%

Political and administrative organisation
Republic composed of 5 regions, 2 autonomous regions, 18 districts, 278 municipalities and 4,051 parishes.

Administrative competence for planning
The government is responsible for the approval of municipal plans, a number of special categories of development which are proposed within protected areas, and the sub-division of land which lies outside of an approved plan. It is also responsible for the planning of major infrastructure projects and for the preparation of regional plans in collaboration with municipal authorities. The municipal authorities are largely responsible for physical planning. Development and Regional Coordination Commissions are responsible to oversee some 60 municipalities each.

Main planning legislation
The spatial planning system is set out in the Urban and Municipal Planning Law 1998; the Compulsory Acquisition Law 1999, and the private Sub-division Law 1999.

Planning and implementation instruments
There is a hierarchical system whereby the government issues statements of national policies for planning and economic development. It is also responsible for major infrastructure projects of national importance such as the national road network, hydraulic works and energy plants. The regional plans provide a framework for the preparation of the local plans, the master plans, and the district plans prepared by the municipal authorities for whole or partial areas. Once a municipal development plan has been approved by the government and the relevant municipal assembly, the authority can proceed to prepare a range of detailed local land use plans. The private sector is entitled to proposed operative urban units in cooperation with municipalities in a joint venture to develop the necessary infrastructure. The same arrangement can be entered for urban regeneration.

Development control
The municipalities are responsible for development control. A building permit has to be obtained before development activity can take place legally. The detailed local land use plans set out the planning standards and requirements which have to be observed by developers.

Planning system in practice
The present system is restrictive and has necessitated the introduction of new legal devices to facilitate public private partnerships. New legal devices were introduced such as the concept of "Strategic Plan". New systems were also put into place for planning implementation and new ways for municipalities to deal with inter-municipality issues by creating metropolitan areas and community areas. Despite intensive and restrictive planning legislation, illegalities such as informal settlements and land divisions are tolerated for political reasons.

Read on: www.min-plan.pt; www.dgotdu.pt; www.dpp.pt; www.aup-spu.org;
http://appla.web.pt; www.civil.ist.utl.pt; http://sigarra.up.pt; www.ua.pt

SLOVAKIA

FAST FACTS

- **Total Area:** 48,845 km^2
- **Total Population:** 5,455,407
- **Population Growth:** 0.143%
- **Unemployment Rate:** 8.6%
- **GDP:** $107.6 billion
- **GDP per capita:** $19,800
- **GDP growth rate:** 8.8%

SETTLEMENTS STRUCTURE

- **Capital City:** Bratislava
  428,800 pop
- **Second City:** Kosice
  233,600 pop
- **Density:** 112 pop/km^2
- **Urban Population:** 58%

Political and administrative organisation
Republic composed of 8 regions, 79 administrative districts and 2,875 municipalities.

Administrative competence for planning
The Ministry of Construction and Regional Development is responsible for the preparation of the national spatial plan. The regional authorities prepare regional plans which have to be approved by the government. The municipal authorities are responsible for the preparation and approval of city master plans, which provide a general spatial framework for the regulation of land use, and detailed zoning plans.

Main planning legislation
The Spatial Planning and Building Act 1976, as amended regularly and most recently in 2003, defines the spatial planning system, the types of plans, and the procedures and regulations that have to be observed when preparing and approving plans. It has established a hierarchical spatial planning system. There is also a building code which establishes spatial planning as an open system easing the implementation of a long term spatial development vision.

Planning and implementation instruments
The National Spatial Development Plan outlines the Government's policies for settlements. It also defines the guiding principles which have to underpin proposals for spatially specific development proposals. The regional plans identify development patterns, including the organisation of land use, and make provision for environmental and nature protection. The city plans set out a general spatial framework for the development and use of land. The zoning plans make provision for the regulation of building plots, building lines, and the height, massing and shape of buildings.

Development control
The municipal authorities are responsible for enforcing development control. The local development and zoning plans set out the planning standards and requirements which developers have to observe when seeking a building permit.

Planning system in practice
Until recently the provisions of national economic plans took precedence over the objectives of spatial planning. The change to a market economy introduced prevention of urban sprawl, the abolishment of prefabricated large scale housing, increased infrastructure, town centre regeneration, and improvement of transportation as part of the 2001 national development perspective. A key goal of spatial planning remains an even territorial distribution of settlements through urban –rural partnerships. Sustainability principles were incorporated in planning to reduce the deterioration of the environment and to protect natural resources. The privatisation of utilities has also an effect on the planning system. The exercise of building control plays an important role in settlement planning and special efforts are made to mobilise the provisions for sustainable tourism, expected to enhance cultural heritage as a development factor.

Read on: www.sazp.sk; www.enviro.gov.sk; www.fa.stuba.sk

FAST FACTS

- **Total Area:** 20,273 km²
- **Total Population:** 2,007,711
- **Population Growth:** -0.088%
- **Unemployment Rate:** 4.6%
- **GDP:** $54.79 billion
- **GDP per capita:** $27,300
- **GDP growth rate:** 5.8%

SETTLEMENTS STRUCTURE

- **Capital City:** Ljubljana
  258,000 pop
- **Second City:** Maribor
  92,400 pop
- **Density:** 99 pop/km²
- **Urban Population:** 59%

Political and administrative organisation
Democratic Parliamentary Republic consisting of 8 regions and 193 local municipalities.

Administrative competence for planning
The state is responsible for planning legislation, the definition of a spatial development strategy, and issuing general guidelines. At present there are no formal regional administrative authorities but the state prepares regional concepts of spatial development with the respective municipalities. The municipal authorities are responsible for the spatial planning and management of their respective territories. They are required to undertake the planning duties set out in the legislation.

Main planning legislation
The Spatial Planning Act 2007 has established a hierarchic system of spatial planning. It also defines the requisite planning regulations and procedures, the types and contents of national and local plans. Provision is made for the joint preparation of regional plans by the government and the municipalities and for inter-municipal plans. The revised Construction Act 2003 re-defined the procedures for obtaining building permits. The Spatial Management Policy of the Republic of Slovenia introduced a new legal system and a market economy.

Planning and implementation instruments
In 2004 the government adopted a spatial development strategy which presented the main planning guidelines, goals and priorities for spatial development, the growth of settlements, infrastructure and landscape. It also set out guidelines for regional and local development and recording of planning data. The regional concept of spatial development prepared jointly by the government and interested municipalities seeks to guide major development projects. The Spatial Order of Slovenia 2004 provides guidance on detailed planning matters. The amended planning act makes local planning compulsory. Local plans consist of general guidelines and the basis for more detailed planning.

Development control
The municipal authorities are responsible for development control, the granting of planning permits and the issue of building permits, which is both expensive and time-consuming.

Planning system in practice
The Assessment of Spatial Development in Slovenia of 2001 constituted the basis of Slovenia's new spatial planning system and was extended to encompass European spatial strategies and international recommendations. Recent changes in the spatial planning system have sought to promote greater flexibility, a speedier implementation process. This may contradict more effective public participation in the decision making process. The transition from integrated economic, social and spatial planning to a normative framework system is yet to prove its worth in practice.

Read on: www.gov.si; www.urbinstitut.si, www.ljudmila.org; www.fgg.uni-lj.si; www.uni-lj.si

SPAIN

FAST FACTS

- **Total Area:** 504,782 km²
- **Total Population:** 40,491,051
- **Population Growth:** 0.096%
- **Unemployment Rate:** 7.6%
- **GDP:** $1.362 trillion
- **GDP per capita:** $33,700
- **GDP growth rate:** 3.8%

SETTLEMENTS STRUCTURE

- **Capital City:** Madrid
  3,169,400 pop
  5,130,000 (metro. area)
- **Second City:** Barcelona
  1,528,800 pop
- **Density:** 80 pop/km²
- **Urban Population:** 77%

Political and administrative organisation

Constitutional monarchy composed of 17 regions, 50 provinces and 8,111 municipalities.

Administrative competence for planning

The state has few legal planning powers save for the preparation of national sectoral plans. The role of the provincial authorities varies depending upon which region they are located in. They have the power to devise planning legislation as well as regional plans and to ratify them. The competences of the provinces vary according to the region they belong to. They can be in charge of drawing up provincial plans and ratifying municipal plans. The municipal authorities are largely responsible for local planning within their respective territories while taking into account contents of upper tier plans.

Main planning legislation

The first spatial planning system was defined in the Land Use Planning Act 1956. Its provisions were last amended in 1992 and in 1998. The Urgent Measures for Liberalisation, 2000 opened up the possibility of building on rural land and to ignore temporary planning programmes to stimulate private development. The new Land Act 2007 abolished these measures and sets up a general framework for sustainable development, land classification, limiting urban growth, house prices and land values.

Planning and implementation instruments

Government departments prepare sectoral plans for communications, agriculture, water, mining, and the protection of special areas. The regional plans establish a framework for the distribution of land uses and activities. The municipal plans make detailed provision for the use and development of land, density, building typologies, land sub-division, environmental protection, sustainability and heritage conservation.

Development control

The municipal authorities are responsible for development control, granting planning permissions and issuing building permits. Developers have to comply with the provisions of all the municipal plans.

Planning system in practice

There is a well-established hierarchy of regional and local plans. The complexity of the implementation and mechanisms and procedures remains a problem. The continued demand of land to support the existing building rate and the speculative process organised around it have been a determinant factor for the local government which found an important source of financing in land qualification. Including more land than required in the local plan and the re-qualification of rural land to accommodate urban activities are common practice. Changes introduced in recent planning legislation such as the delimitation of urban land according to the needs of cities, new criteria for the evaluation of land focusing on existing land use rather than expectations of land uses owing to planning and the adoption of sustainable development principles should improve the quality of life in cities and their surroundings. It is too early to judge though.

Read on: www.fomento.es, www.mma.es; www.femp.es; www.aetu.es;

SWEDEN

FAST FACTS

- **Total Area:** 449,964 km²
- **Total Population:** 9,045,389
- **Population Growth:** 0.157%
- **Unemployment Rate:** 4.5%
- **GDP:** $333.1 billion
- **GDP per capita:** $36,900
- **GDP growth rate:** 3.4%

SETTLEMENTS STRUCTURE

- **Capital City:** Stockholm
  1,251,900 pop
  1,622,300 (metro area)
- **Second City:** Göteborg
  506,600 pop
- **Density:** 20 pop/km²
- **Urban Population:** 83%

126

Political and administrative organisation
Constitutional monarchy composed of 21 counties and 290 municipalities.

Administrative competence for planning
The government prepares policies for national physical planning and building matters, and for the provision of housing. The National Board of Housing, Building and Planning monitors developments in respect of physical planning, building codes and permits, and the provision of housing. The county councils are responsible for regional planning and coordinating the activities of their constituent municipalities. The municipalities are responsible for certain planning matters and decisions on minor cases.

Main planning legislation
The National Resources Act, the Planning and Building Act 1987 and the Environmental Code 1999 have replaced the old planning system, laying more emphasis on environmental matters which have equal status with spatial development. These laws encourage the long term management of land and water in ecological, social and economic terms by respecting the public interest as well as individual freedoms. They set out the objectives and procedures for spatial development planning. Legislation on heritage conservation and expropriation extends the role of planning.

Planning and implementation instruments
National planning guidance is set out in the sectoral plans prepared by government departments. In exceptional cases municipalities can collaborate to prepare regional plans. The county councils provide specialist inputs to the municipal plans. The structure plans, special area plans and detailed plans prepared by the municipalities make provision for the development and use of land. Certain government development activities have deemed planning permission.

Development control
The municipalities are responsible for determining applications for changes of use, for the demolition of buildings, and the development and use of land and buildings. Developers are expected to have regard to environmental, health and safety considerations and need to respect any precedents.

Planning system in practice
The existing planning system has been revised to meet the requirements of sustainable development and facilitate the achievement of national goals for the environment. A new regulatory framework for the technical performance of buildings and physical structures has been put into place. This includes renewable energy generation and other energy efficiency measures for buildings. A number of other measures were proposed which reach beyond development control and deals with building and the public realm in use, including responsibilities for maintenance. More efficiency is expected from better coordination between sectors and over time during the planning process. Public participation is encouraged through greater transparency of the planning process.

Read on: www.sweden.gov.se; www.nordregio.se; www.formas.se; www.planering.org;

UNITED KINGDOM

Political and administrative organisation
Constitutional monarchy composed of England, Northern Ireland, Scotland and Wales. In addition to the Scottish Parliament and Welsh Assembly there is a complex system of county, district and unitary authorities.

Administrative competence for planning
Government control over the planning system is exercised by the Department of Communities and Local Government in England, the Scottish Executive, and the Northern Ireland and Welsh Assemblies. In each case the respective local authorities are responsible for plan making and the exercise of planning powers. Planning is administered through a combination of central and local government. In England, the Greater London Authority is the regional planning body for Greater London, although not directly elected.

Main planning legislation
There is separate planning legislation for England, Northern Ireland, Scotland and Wales. The Town and Country Planning Act 1990, as amended in 1991 and 2004, establishes the planning system for England and Wales. The main planning legislation in Scotland is the Town and Country Planning (Scotland) Act 1997. In Northern Ireland planning is ruled by the Planning (Northern Ireland) Order 1972 and the Planning Reform (Northern Ireland) Order 2006.

Planning and implementation instruments
Statements of national and regional policy have been prepared for England, Northern Ireland, Scotland and Wales. National spatial exist in Northern Ireland, Scotland and Wales. The dual purpose of spatial planning is to regulate development and use of land in the public interest, and to contribute to the achievement of sustainable development. The development plans prepared by local authorities set out their policies and proposals for meeting the economic, environmental and social aims for their areas. There are either two tier county and municipal plans or unitary development plans in single tier local authorties. Usually the plans contain a planning framework or a policy statement and a land use and implementation plan.

Development control
Planning legislation defines development requiring planning permission. Certain categories of development proposals are subject to environmental impact assessment. Local authorities are responsible for determining planning applications.

Planning system in practice
The UK planning system's achievements have been considerable. The reform of the English planning system in 2004 has proved difficult to implement. Further reforms are currently set out in the Planning Bill introduced at the end of 2007. Meanwhile, the land use and settlement pattern remains highly car dependent, wit urban sprawl of housing and many other activities, such as regional shopping centres, logistics, and business parks. A recent trend is to return to the use of brownfield sites to encourage more compact cities and higher densities facilitating public transport use.

Read on: www.communities.gov.uk; www.defra.gov.uk; www.environment-agency.gov.uk;

FAST FACTS
- **Total Area:** 244,820 km²
- **Total Population:** 60,943,912
- **Population Growth:** 0.276%
- **Unemployment Rate:** 5.4%
- **GDP:** $2.147 trillion
- **GDP per capita:** $35,300
- **GDP growth rate:** 2.9%

SETTLEMENTS STRUCTURE
- **Capital City:** London
  7,429,200 pop
  7,615,000 (metro area)
- **Second City:** Glasgow
  1,099,400 pop
- **Density:** 249 pop/km²
- **Urban Population:** 89%

FAST FACTS

- **Total Area:** 103,000 km²
- **Total Population:** 304,367
- **Population Growth:** 0.783%
- **Unemployment Rate:** 1%
- **GDP:** $11.89 billion
- **GDP per capita:** $39,400
- **GDP growth rate:** 1.8%

SETTLEMENTS STRUCTURE

- **Capital City:** Reykjavik
  114,800 pop
  184,200 (metro area)
- **Second City:** Akureyri
  17,304 pop
- **Density:** 3 pop/km²
- **Urban Population:** 93%

Political and administrative organisation
Republic composed of 8 regions, 6 regional constituencies, 23 counties and 79 municipalities.

Administrative competence for planning
The Minister for the Environment is responsible for planning and building. The regions do not have any executive functions. The municipalities which have been reduced from over 200 to 79 to provide more effective services are empowered to prepare regional and local development plans and they are in charge of development control. A Planning and Building Tribunal appointed by the Minister resolves disputes on planning and building matters.

Main planning legislation
The Planning and Building Act 1997 defines the statutory planning system and related building regulations. The local authorities are empowered to prepare municipal and detailed local development plans.

Planning and implementation instruments
The Minister for the Environment is responsible for co-ordinating sectoral plans and is empowered to direct that local authorities have regard to any guidance that is issued. Although there is no provision for the preparation of regional plans two or more local authorities can agree to prepare a regional plan.

Development control
The municipalities are responsible for development control and are empowered to issue building permits and development permits, and carry out building and enforcement inspections. Development proposals must conform with the provisions of the relevant local development plan.

Planning system in practice
Disagreements between central and local government and between individual local authorities have highlighted the need for some form of national land use strategy and guidelines. It is envisaged that in future the Planning Agency will present an annual national planning policy paper to the Minister. This will be submitted to Parliament. Once approved its provisions must be observed by local authorities. The new Planning Act has taken effect on the 1st of January 2008 with expected ensuing changes in the planning system and its implementation. The Strategic Environmental Assessment Directive, providing guidance for planning authorities of the European Union, is expected to be a support for the modernisation of the future planning system in Iceland. As it encompasses a wide range of plans and programmes, including town and country planning and land use the Directive will apply to present and future planning systems, and in particular, to regional planning guidance, local development documents and regional spatial strategies as well as current and proposed development plans. Environmental issues are of particular importance to Iceland with its fragile ecology and large scale often external development pressure to continue to establish polluting manufacturing plants, oil terminals and refineries which Iceland with its large amount of indigenous renewable energy does not need.

Read on: www.umhverfisraduneyti.is

NORWAY 🇳🇴

FAST FACTS

- **Total Area:** 323,802 km²
- **Total Population:** 4,644,457
- **Population Growth:** 0.35%
- **Unemployment Rate:** 2.4%
- **GDP:** $257.4 billion
- **GDP per capita:** $55,600
- **GDP growth rate:** 4.9%

SETTLEMENTS STRUCTURE

- **Capital City:** Oslo
  791,500 pop
- **Second City:** Bergen
  211,200 pop
- **Density:** 14 pop/km²
- **Urban Population:** 81%

Political and administrative organisation
Constitutional monarchy composed of 19 counties and 435 municipalities.

Administrative competence for planning
The state is responsible for defining the spatial planning system and monitoring its operation at county and municipal levels. The county councils are responsible for coordinating major planning activities within their respective jurisdictions. The municipalities are responsible for local planning and development control. The state is also drawing up sectoral plans, including for oil exploration and distribution and related environmental protection which constitutes an important part of spatial development.

Main planning legislation
The Planning and Building Act 1985 defines and regulates the operation of the spatial planning and building system at all levels of government, including the regulation of all building activity. The Act includes Environment Impact Assessments and other by-laws and the Ministry of the Environment has to be notified of spatial and building developments. Complementary planning powers in respect of nature conservation, farm land and recreation are set out in other Acts.

Planning and implementation instruments
The Ministry of Environment issues comprehensive guidelines which set out the national objectives and expectations of government departments. It also issues policy guidelines for specific aspects of planning activity. The county plans identify long-term objectives and policy guidelines for regional development in each county. The municipal comprehensive plans make provision for local community development and services. The local development plans regulate the use, development and protection of land. The building development plans set out regulations for the design of buildings. Comprehensive planning ensures coordination between the three planning levels. It also provides a framework for the balanced physical, economic and socio-cultural development throughout the country.

Development control
The municipal authorities are responsible for issuing building permits and ensuring that development proposals observe the detailed regulations and requirements set out in approved plans. All building activity must comply with requirements of access, water supply and sewage treatment.

Planning system in practice
The planning system is currently being reviewed to ensure that it is more adaptable to changing needs. Central government has too many guidelines for the county and municipal planning, not leaving sufficient scope for regional and local policies. Certain sector plans and sector decisions are also superseding the comprehensive planning undertaken by county councils and municipalities. The mechanisms for co-ordinating spatial planning across municipal boundaries are not sufficient. Municipalities are to an increasing extent granting exemptions from their own enforced plans which tends to undermine the planning system.

Read on: www.regjeringen.no; www.norad.no; www.uio.no; www.ntnu.no; www.hivolda.no

FAST FACTS

- **Total Area:** 41,290 km²
- **Total Population:** 7,581,520
- **Population Growth:** 0.329%
- **Unemployment Rate:** 3.1%
- **GDP:** $300.9 billion
- **GDP per capita:** $39,800
- **GDP growth rate:** 2.6%

SETTLEMENTS STRUCTURE

- **Capital City:** Bern
  122,700 pop
- **Second City:** Zurich
  348,100 pop
- **Density:** 184 pop/km²
- **Urban Population:** 68%

Political and administrative organisation
Federal republic composed of 26 regions (cantons) and 2,865 municipalities.

Administrative competence for planning
The Federal Council is responsible for national spatial co-ordination, the co-ordination of sector plans and for the approval of the structure plans prepared by the cantons. The cantons are the main planning authority. They are able to draw up their own planning legislation and physical planning strategies and plans. The municipalities have also the possibility to draw up planning regulations and are responsible for the preparation of land use plans and their ratification, and can draw up their own building regulations and control them.

Main planning legislation
Since 1969, the federal level has the responsibility of coordination, including for spatial planning. The Federal Spatial Planning Acts 1980 and 1990 set out the legal framework for land use planning. Their provisions are complemented by legislation on motorways, railways, aviation, water pollution, environmental protection, housing, regional policy and tourism. In addition there are the planning and building laws passed by the cantons and the communes respectively, which have to pass a public referendum.

Planning and implementation instruments
There is no comprehensive national plan. The cantons prepare structure plans which provide guidance for spatial development. The municipalities prepare district-wide land use plans which are binding on land owners. In the case of important projects the cantons can prepare land use plans replacing parts of plans prepared by the municipalities. In large cantons, supra-municipal spatial planning tasks can be delegated to public planning associations at the regional level which may draw up regional structure plans or provide analytical inputs to plans drawn up by the local authorities.

Development control
The municipalities are responsible for development and land use control, as well as for the enforcement of building control and regulations.

Planning system in practice
The various public bodies and agencies consider that spatial co-ordination gives rise to obstacles and delays. There are considerable variations in the planning and building requirements adopted by the cantons. A public referendum has made it possible for agricultural land to be developed for other purposes. This will result in increased development pressure in the fringe areas of metropolitan cities. During the unexpected economic recession in the seventies, planning was reduced to short term problem solving and lost its role to devise comprehensive spatial development concepts. This was redressed and both structure planning and horizontal coordination with continuous updating were reintroduced in the 1980 Act. Public participation occupies a greater role despite fears of delays and contributes to a decentralised, polycentric settlement strategy.

Read on: www.are.admin.ch; www.bafu.admin.ch; www.vlp.ch; www.sia.ch;

ALBANIA

FAST FACTS

- **Total Area:** 28,748 km²
- **Total Population:** 3,619,778
- **Population Growth:** 0.538%
- **Unemployment Rate:** 13%
- **GDP:** $19.76 billion
- **GDP per capita:** $5,500
- **GDP growth rate:** 5%

SETTLEMENTS STRUCTURE

- **Capital City:** Tirana
  353,400 pop

- **Second City:** Durres
  113,900 pop

- **Density:** 126 pop/km²

- **Urban Population:** 45%

Political and administrative organisation

Republic composed of 12 counties, 36 districts, municipalities and communes.

Administrative competence for planning

Three levels are involved in what remains a very centralised system. The national council of territorial adjustment approves most plans while the National Planning Institute is de facto producing all the plans. The regional and the municipal councils of territorial adjustment have limited powers. Coordination is the task of the Department of Urban Development and Territorial Planning.

Main planning legislation

The main laws are the Urban Planning Law 1998, postulating land use regulation based on zoning; the Government Decree on Urban Planning Regulations 1999; the Law on Organisation and Functioning of Local Government 2000; and the Law on Construction Police 1998, effectively development control.

Planning and implementation instruments

Land privatisation took place in 1992. Land use planning is carried out at the lowest level by municipalities (towns and cities) and communes (rural villages) which are also in charge of housing and land management according to the principles of decentralisation introduced after the abandonment of communism. Plans include a national master plan, regional and municipal plans for their respective areas and local area plans for specific uses. The planning process is very normative and prescriptive, operating with obsolete rigid mechanisms predating the adopted market system.

Development control

A two tier development control mechanisms is enforcing the conformity of planning and issuing development permits. Despite strict planning rules, much informal development occurs, mainly housing, despite lack of basic infrastructure.

Planning system in practice

There is a great gap between the planning system and the development in reality. While political, social and economic life entered a new era, the planning system continued to operate with obsolete instruments, rigid top down planning without local adaptation and ineffective implementation or enforcement mechanisms, unable to control the massive sprawl of Tirane. . Contradiction between planning and local government legislation and lack of regulations for land division and readjustment hamper local development processes. Extreme centralisation prevails, thus decentralised institutions are ill equipped to realise community based development and enforce the planning laws. Involvement of any users in the planning decisions, other than government officials has been minimal or non-existent, except when NGOs supported by international development aid are involved. There is also a serious lack of resources for planning and infrastructure provision to accommodate planned urban growth.

Read on: www.pad.gov.al; www.unitir.edu.al; www.umar.org/rubrique215.html

ARMENIA

FAST FACTS

- **Total Area:** 29 800 km²
- **Total Population:** 2,968,586
- **Population Growth:** -0.077%
- **Unemployment Rate:** 7.1%
- **GDP:** $16.83 billion
- **GDP per capita:** $5,700
- **GDP growth rate:** 13.7%

SETTLEMENTS STRUCTURE

- **Capital City:** Yerevan
  1,267,600 pop
  1,462,700 (metro area)
- **Second City:** Vanadzor
  147,400 pop
- **Density:** 100 pop/km²
- **Urban Population:** 64%

Political and administrative organisation

Republic composed of 11 provinces (mazes) and self governing communities.

Administrative competence for planning

The Urban Development Ministry is in charge of devising the national plan. It supervises lower tiers of planning, securing vertical compatibility. The State Urban Development Inspectorate controls compliance of development activities with planning legislation. The state governors oversee and/or carry out planning at regional level (marzes). Despite decentralisation the marzes have still limited planning powers. The self-governing local communes are responsible for statutory local planning and development control. They have property and economic rights and can set local taxes. The capital Yerecan is a community with its own peculiarities laid down by law.

Main planning legislation

Law on Urban Development 1998 and amended in 2000 and 2005; Law on Responsibility for violation of rights in the sphere of Urban Development, Housing Law; Law on responsibilities of participants in urban development activities; Resolutions regulating the competences, plan making process and types of plans and information.

Planning and implementation instruments

Plans are established at three levels. At the national level there exists a spatial strategy and settlement structure; a housing strategy and guidance for sustainable development and infrastructures. At the regional level there are spatial development strategies and programmes;. The commune level is in charge of statutory master plans, land use plans and detailed zoning plans which include transport and communication plans. Plans are based on detailed analyses of local physical, socio-economic, cultural and environmental conditions and have to be regularly updated. Allowances are made to facilitate foreign investment in real estate property and development, including construction companies.

Development control

It is carried out by the communes, controlled by a state inspectorate also in charge of compliance with the law. Public participation is embedded in the planning laws.

Planning system in practice

Considering recent independence from the Soviet Union in 1991, centralised structures remain in place despite a will to devolve responsibilities, including for planning to the lowest level. Communes lack technical and personnel capacity as well as operational finance. They are thus limited in carrying out planning activities and have difficulties to deal with illegal settlements. Capacity building is necessary for democratic reasons which also emphasise public participation and involvement of key local and regional actors from civil society and business. Armenia is aligning its planning system on the ESDP and endorses UN sustainable development principles.

Read on: www.gov.am; www.yeriac.iatp.irex.am; http://spyur.am/archunion.htm

AZERBAIJAN

FAST FACTS

- **Total Area:** 86,000 km²
- **Total Population:** 8.177.717
- **Population Growth:** 0.723%
- **Unemployment Rate:** 4.3%
- **GDP:** $65.47 billion
- **GDP per capita:** $7,700
- **GDP growth rate:** 23.4%

SETTLEMENTS STRUCTURE

- **Capital City:** Baku
  1,235,400 pop
  2,118,600 (metro. area)
- **Second City:** Ganja
  303,000 pop
- **Density:** 95 pop/km²
- **Urban Population:** 50%

Political and administrative organisation
Republic composed of 59 districts (rayons), 11 cities and 1 autonomous republic (Naxcivan Muxtar).

Administrative competence for planning
The state retains strong central powers overall, including the planning and development system. It regulates land tenure. The State Committee for Construction and Architecture is in charge of spatial policy formulation, drafting laws on planning, architecture and construction. The state imposes sectoral policies affecting spatial development, such as transportation, energy distribution, etc. There is a strict planning hierarchy, but since 1999 regions and municipalities are responsible for drawing up plans at their respective levels which need central ratification. Planning in relation to natural disasters, pollution and nature protection are directed by the state. The country attaches great importance to environmental protection which influences spatial planning.

Main planning legislation
The Town Planning Act 1999 and the Architectural Act 1998 regulate spatial planning and development. They aim at optimum population distribution and lay down standards for planning and construction. A number of articles of the criminal code devise norms and penalties for building, especially on the coast. The 1999 Law on the Status of Municipalities gives lower tier administrations planning powers. The 2000 Law on NGOs enables them to participate more actively in the spatial development process. Decrees regulate payment for the use of natural resources. The 1992 law on environmental protection and nature utilisation influences spatial development in a country with severe pollution problems.

Planning and implementation instruments
Implementation of spatial strategies is ruled by state budgets. The state also prepares a national spatial strategy, together with development and implementation regulations of government policies, and regulates the supervision of the observance of standards. It also has prepared a national environmental action plan and nature protection plans. Local architecture and building committees mirror the national one and carry out similar tasks including plan making, but under state control.

Development control
Development control is carried out locally but supervised by the state. Participation is weak but measures are planning to improve the involvement of the local population in the development of their areas.

Planning system in practice
While environmental planning seems strong, physical planning remains underdeveloped and strongly controlled from the centre. Local participation is not encouraged, except for house building. The transition to the market economy is not completed and with less instability in the region more foreign investment may well transform spatial development.

Read on: www.economy.gov.az; www.khazar.org

133

FAST FACTS

- **Total Area:** 51,129 km²
- **Total Population:** 4,590,310
- **Population Growth:** 0.666%
- **Unemployment Rate:** 45.5%
- **GDP:** $29.89 billion
- **GDP per capita:** $6,600
- **GDP growth rate:** 5.5%

SETTLEMENTS STRUCTURE

- **Capital City:** Sarajevo
  581,500 pop
- **Second City:** Banja Luka
  189,700 pop
- **Density:** 90 pop/km²
- **Urban Population:** 45%

Political and administrative organisation

Bosnia and Herzegovina has adopted a unique new form of state after the civil war from 1992 – 1995 with two administrative entities: the Federation of Bosnia and Herzegovina (BiH) and the Republic of Srpska, as well as a district with special status. The BiH Federation consists of 10 cantons and 79 municipalities. Srpska is unitary with 62 municipalities.

Administrative competence for planning

No administrative competence for planning exists at state level. The Federation of BiH, the Srpska Republic and the Brcko District are responsible for planning and housing through their respective planning ministries. Their competences vary but they are able to devise planning legislation, except in the BiH Federation where the cantons have considerable planning authority. Municipalities often related to ethnic concentrations devise land use plans on ethnic lines. Overall administrative structure and responsibilities vary considerably between the different parts of the Federation.

Main planning legislation

The National Law on Spatial Development, land and land ownership was imposed by the UN High Representative. In the BiH Federation, there exists a law on federal planning and land development, laws on housing, environmental protection and waste. Regulations remain from previous times on cadastre and real estate from 1984, usurpations from 1978, and designation of construction land in urban settlements from 1968. Srpska has a new law on spatial regulation, housing, environmental protection construction. The Brcko district law defines its statute, land rights, spatial regulation, measures against illegal settlements. There is no national development coordination by law.

Planning and implementation instruments

In the BiH Federation there exists a federal spatial strategy, development plans at cantonal level, land use, detail plans for urbanising areas and urban projects. There is no overall development strategy in Srbska or Brcko.

Development control

After the demise of communism, civil war, independence and transition both development control and public participation are at the lowest level. They are not yet clearly defined, with old practices still in operation.

Planning system in practice

The new complex system is in danger of facilitating bypass tactics as the procedures are long, cumbersome, with confusing division of responsibilities without overall spatial development coordination. Greater public participation needs to be reincorporated into a planning system with simplified procedures and better coordination between the various types of local plans and regulations. Little evidence is underpinning the spatial development strategies proposed at various uncoordinated levels, despite the complex entanglement of the various authorities. Urban development plans are devised in isolation where intense construction activity Is expected.

Read on: www.fmpu.gov.ba; www.unsa.ba/eng/arhitektura.php; www.unibl.rs.sr

CROATIA

FAST FACTS

- **Total Area:** 56,542 km²
- **Total Population:** 4,491,543
- **Population Growth:** -0.043%
- **Unemployment Rate:** 11.8%
- **GDP:** $69.44 billion
- **GDP per capita:** $15,500
- **GDP growth rate:** 5.6%

SETTLEMENTS STRUCTURE

- **Capital City:** Zagreb
  685,500 pop
- **Second City:** Split
  173,600 pop
- **Density:** 79 pop/km²
- **Urban Population:** 60%

Political and administrative organisation
Republic composed of 21 counties, the city of Zagreb and many districts.

Administrative competence for planning
The state is responsible for the operation of the planning system, and the formulation and enforcement of the planning regulations and instruments. It is also responsible for the enforcement of these rules. The Croatian Parliament is responsible for approving national protected park plans and major infrastructure projects. The Ministry of Environmental Protection and Physical Planning ensures that the plans and policies have been formally approved and adopted by the appropriate local authorities. The county and district authorities are empowered to prepare, as appropriate, regional and local plans.

Main planning legislation
The republic has inherited the former Yugoslavian regional and urban planning system. The Physical Planning Law defines the present planning system. Its provisions are developed in greater detail in the Implementation Rule Book. The provisions of the legislation on environmental, nature and air quality protection, agriculture and forestry have also to be taken into account when plans are prepared.

Planning and implementation instruments
There is a hierarchy of planning instruments which consists of the national, regional and district plans prepared respectively by the government, county and district planning departments. The districts can also be directed to prepare town plans and master plans.

Development control
The municipal authorities are responsible for the exercise of planning control over the development and use of land. This task has been made difficult by the lack of legally enforceable, site specific land use zoning and density standards. Development pressures in the major cities and along the Adriatic coast have resulted in much illegal development.

Planning system in practice
Development pressures are creating serious problems for planning at all levels. Illegal development is twofold: illegal settlements due to the urbanisation process and constructions for tourims mainly on the coast. Many of the municipal authorities do not have the resources to operate an overcomplex and slow planning system. Thus only half the country is covered by regional plans, which are lacking especially in less attractive areas. New building can take place on green fields and whole existing settlements can be destroyed or their uses changed without planning permission. Land use categories are not clarifed in the planning legislation. A particular problem is that levies earmarked for infrastructure cannot be spent in advance of the main development while there are no provisions for the private sector to invest directly in infrastructure of their developments. The land market is not functioning due to remains of the previous regime and reluctance of the public sector to participate in land transactions.

Read on: www.mzopu.hr; www.arhitekt.hr

GEORGIA

FAST FACTS

- **Total Area:** 69,700 km²
- **Total Population:** 4,630,841
- **Population Growth:** -0.325%
- **Unemployment Rate:** 50%
- **GDP:** $19.65 billion
- **GDP per capita:** $4,200
- **GDP growth rate:** 12%

SETTLEMENTS STRUCTURE

- **Capital City:** Tbilisi
  1,240,200 pop
  1,440,000 (metro. area)
- **Second City:** Kutaisi
  268,800 pop
- **Density:** 66 pop/km²
- **Urban Population:** 52%

Political and administrative organisation

Republic composed of 11 administrative regions, including Ajarian Autonomous Republic and the Abkhazian Autonomous Republic, as well as 69 districts.

Administrative competence for planning

The government of a highly centralised state except for the autonomous republics is responsible for national and regional planning. The Department of Urbanisation and Construction is responsible for urban planning, housing, infrastructure, construction and licenses. Policies for transport, communications, tourism, urbanisation and construction are formulated by the Ministry of Economic Development which includes urban development, transportation, urbanisation, construction and privatisation. Local authorities are solely responsible for local land use plans.

Main planning legislation

The following Acts encompass aspects of planning: Environmental Protection 1996, Area Protection 1996, Cultural Heritage 1999, Construction Permits 2004 and Licences and Permits 2005. The latest statutory provisions are set out in the Backgrounds of Space Arrangements and City Planning Law 2005.

Planning and implementation instruments

It is envisaged that there will be a hierarchy of nation, regional and local development plans. At present there are no national and regional plans. Most cities have not, as yet, prepared master plans and detailed local development plans. Some cities have defined land use and building zones which set out their planning and construction requirements. The private sector is very active, mainly in commercial housing construction with little planning control. Public participation is minimal.

Development control

The State favours a liberal market economy approach and is only responsible for approving major projects. It has also abolished construction licences. Most applications are dealt with by the local authorities. There is much illegal construction activity.

Planning system in practice

After transition from a state planned to a market economy the present system requires further reform. In the absence of a national spatial strategy the urban landscape has suffered from uncontrolled development and destruction of heritage. The most problematic issue is the absence of a coherent legislative package of norms, rules and standards. Laws, President's Decrees and other by-laws were only declared, but not enforced as they were not supported financially, institutionally, and most importantly, politically. These measures have failed to control new development and land use changes. The public has little contact with, and interest in the planning system. There is a lack of technical and financial support for evidence based planning.

Read on: www.economy.gov.ge; www.garemo.itdc.ge;
http://arcunion.iatp.org.ge/index_ge.html; www.gtu.edu.ge; www.tesau.edu.ge

FAST FACTS

- **Total Area:** 10,887 km²
- **Total Population:** 2,126,708
- **Population Growth:** -
- **Unemployment Rate:** 43%
- **GDP:** $4 billion
- **GDP per capita:** $1,800
- **GDP growth rate:** 2.6%

SETTLEMENTS STRUCTURE

- **Capital City:** Pristina
  206,686 pop
- **Second City:** Prizren
  127,020 pop
- **Density:** 195 pop/km²
- **Urban Population:** -

Political and administrative organisation
Unilaterally declared independence. Republic under UN interim administration composed of 30 municipalities.

Administrative competence for planning
There are two levels of planning, national and local. Since 2002 the new Ministry of Environment and Spatial Planning (MESP) is in charge of national planning provision and policy formulation, guidance for municipalities and ensuring public participation. 30 local authorities are responsible for planning, and proposing regulations and procedures at municipal level, together with implementing national legislation. Respectively, these bodies will obtain professional assistance by the future Spatial Planning Council and the Committees of Planning Experts appointed by the municipal assembly.

Main planning legislation
Spatial Planning Law 2003.

Planning and implementation instruments
MESP produces the Kosovo national plan, the strategy for spatial development in Kosovo. It issues guidelines and policy documents also for local planning, which it coordinates nationally, assisting with databases, harmonising local plans and monitoring planning nationwide. The Institute for Spatial Planning elaborates a national plan based on its research. Municipalities prepare a multi-sectoral municipal spatial, economic and social development plan, an urban development plan and urban regulatory plans. They also implement national guidelines and manage local projects. Most of these institutions and their tasks are new and their workings will require adjustment in practice, without benfiting from a preset monitoring process.

Development control
National planning inspectors oversee the overall implementation of planning law while municipal construction inspectors ensure compliance of development with the plans and enforce locally set penalties.

Planning system in practice
Recently introduced, the new planning system is still in its experimental stage and produces finite plans rather than a dynamic process. Planning authorities, at both levels, don't have sufficient capacities to manage the planning processes. This is a consequence of the main obstacles that institutions are facing. However, contracting planning out to private firms may give rise to abuse if the planning authority leaves all its responsibilities entirely in the hands of outsiders. Current planning is undergoing an elaborate participation process which may be the basis for a new, more bottom up departure for planning and development, although it may lack a future oriented approach. At the local level participation is more akin to consultation at the end of the planning process which may hamper implementation. Countries like Kosovo who are undergoing profound transformations may present the opportunity to leading the way to innovative planning processes.

Read on: www.ks-gov.net; www.komunat-ks.net; www.uni-pr.edu

FAST FACTS

- **Total Area:** 25,333 km²
- **Total Population:** 2,061,315
- **Population Growth:** 0.262%
- **Unemployment Rate:** 35%
- **GDP:** $17.35 billion
- **GDP per capita:** $8,500
- **GDP growth rate:** 5%

SETTLEMENTS STRUCTURE

- **Capital City:** Skopje
  452,500 pop
  587,300 (metro. area)
- **Second City:** Bitola
  84,400 pop
- **Density:** 81 pop/km²
- **Urban Population:** 60%

Political and administrative organisation
Republic composed of 84 municipalities grouped into 8 statistical regions.

Administrative competence for planning
The Republic Ministry of Environment and Physical Planning (RMEPP) is the main central government body responsible for environmental management and spatial planning. The 2002 Law on Local Self-Government transferred power to the municipalities including, among several matters, public services, environment, urban and rural planning, economic development and local finance.

Main planning legislation
The main piece of contemporary planning legislation is the Spatial and Urban Planning Act, 2005, that covers basically two distinctive phases: plan preparation and plan adoption.

Planning and implementation instruments
Central government and local communes are involved in the preparation and implementation of the spatial plans of the republic, regions and special purpose areas, as well as on different types of urban plans (e.g. master or general urban plan, detailed urban plan, village urban plan and settlement urban plan). The central government launches annual programmes of planning preparations. A similar situation is found at the local level where the financing and duration of planning is regulated by communal programmes, except for the city of Skopje that has a special planning programme.

Development control
The approaches to planning implementation are based on traditional instruments such as a land use and construction diagram, an urban project, and building permit. The first two are more technical documents than implementation tools, bridging the gap between plan preparation and plan implementation. The absence of development and building control codes, zoning overlays and ordinances, conservation easements, impact fees, density bonus and many other tools make planning implementation difficult.

Planning system in practice
The existing planning system in Macedonia is still in the stage of searching solutions for directing and controlling spatial development within the newly created socio-economic and political conditions. Unfortunately, the solutions offered through legislation and planning practice are not in compliance with the resulting changes, nor very distant from the socialist period. Several challenges have to be attended: the implementation of western-type development, currently unsupported by an adequate legislative and professional base; the lack of technology and infrastructure; the improvement of local human resources, of those already involved in planning as well as of future generations of planners; the stimulation of the public to participate in planning processes; and the inclusion in planning of areas such as the issue of gender, social exclusion and inclusion, minority rights and vulnerable groups, trans-border area planning, and others.

Read on: www.moepp.gov.mk; www.ukim.edu.mk

FAST FACTS

- **Total Area:** 17,075,200 km²
- **Total Population:** 140,702,094
- **Population Growth:** -0.474%
- **Unemployment Rate:** 5.9%
- **GDP:** $2.076 trillion
- **GDP per capita:** $14,600
- **GDP growth rate:** 8.1%

SETTLEMENTS STRUCTURE

- **Capital City:** Moscow
  10,101,500 pop
  10,672,000 (metro. area)
- **Second City:** St-Petersburg
  4,582,300 pop
- **Density:** 8 pop/km²
- **Urban Population:** 73%

Political and administrative organisation
Federal Republic composed of 89 regions, 21 republics, 49 provinces, 6 territories, 10 autonomous districts, 1 autonomous province, 2 federal cities and municipalities.

Administrative competence for planning
The state is responsible for national spatial planning. The Federal Housing and Construction Agency prepares territorial planning schemes. The federal and regional authorities are responsible for undertaking regional territorial planning. The municipalities are empowered to prepare master plans, zoning regulations and detailed layout guidance.

Main planning legislation
The Federal Planning Law 1992 defined the nature, purpose and role of the planning system. The New Planning Code 2004 has issued new requirements in respect of territorial planning, zoning regulations and layout guidance. The Federal Planning Law 2005 has reorganised the administrative divisions, powers and responsibilities. A complex system of federal, regional and municipal laws makes provisions for the preparation of land use plans.

Planning and implementation instruments
The state issues national territorial planning schemes which set out planning goals and objectives. However there is no single national spatial development perspective. The regional authorities issue schemes for the planned development of protected natural landscape, for regional infrastructure, and agricultural land boundary changes. The municipal authorities prepare development schemes. The urban and rural districts prepare explanatory land use statements and zoning regulations.

Development control
The local authorities are responsible for the issue of building permits. Each level of local government is allowed to develop land under its control.

Planning system in practice
The new planning system has not been in operation long enough to provide evidence based feedback. However, in recent years the planning system was unable to cope with major land use change which resulted from rapid economic growth. The resources at the disposal of each local authority will determine the effectiveness of the new system. A particular problem is the sprawl of second homes into protected nature areas, as well as other infringements on cultural heritage. This is less due to lack of planning documentation than to lack of understanding of social and market forces and arbitrary decisions under pressure which have led to some inappropriate large scale developments, thereby highlighting problems of governance in general. During the recent period of urban development, a lot of investment was able to improve physical as well as socio-economic infrastructure in a planned, coordinated manner. The rational to strengthen the national and the local level to the detriment of the regional level seems to run counter general trends.

Read on: www.flc.ru; www.kadastr.ru; www.uar.ru; www.klgtu.ru; www.geogr.msu.ru; www.novsu.ac.ru; www.gasa.krs.ru

SERBIA

FAST FACTS

- **Total Area:** 77,474 km²
- **Total Population:** 10,159,046
- **Population Growth:** -
- **Unemployment Rate:** 18.8%
- **GDP:** $56.89 billion
- **GDP per capita:** $7,700
- **GDP growth rate:** 7%

SETTLEMENTS STRUCTURE

- **Capital City:** Belgrade
  1,285,200 pop
  1,717,800 (metro. area)
- **Second City:** Novi Sad
  191,300 pop
- **Density:** 131 pop/km²
- **Urban Population:** 52%

Political and administrative organisation
Republic composed of 2 autonomous regions, 25 counties and 190 districts.

Administrative competence for planning
The government is responsible for the establishment of a new planning system. The Ministry of Infrastructure is in charge of urban and spatial planning. The Ministries responsible for Environmental Protection, Agriculture, Forestry and Water Management contribute as appropriate to the preparation of national and regional plans. The municipalities are empowered to prepare both general and detailed land use plans, and appoint a chief architect to monitor, implement and modify plans.

Main planning legislation
Local authorities can now play a more important role in respect of the formulation of development programmes and strategies, urban planning and budgets as a result of the reforms introduced by the Self Governance Act 2002. The Planning and Construction Act 2003 has established a new system of spatial plans and urban plans. It has simplified procedures and codified the law on land ownership, property rights, and made provision for the legalisation of some illegal settlement development.

Planning and implementation instruments
It is envisaged that there will be a hierarchy of planning instruments. It will consist of a national spatial development strategy, regional sectoral development strategies, while the municipal authorities prepare master plans, general development plans and regulatory plans, as well as urban design projects to guide the division of land into building plots.

Development control
Developers have to submit details of land ownership, construction, layout, design, proposed use, cost and value of the development when applying for a building permit. Development control is the task of municipalities.

Planning system in practice
The planning system is still evolving. It has a long history of extraneous influences which are embedded in the existing built environment. However, proscribed changes to land management policy, re-privatising land nationalised under communism and the status of building land in cities are not implemented in practice. Although not all local governance issues are covered yet by new legislation some municipalities have not welcomed the challenge presented by decentralisation, whilst others are adopting a more flexible and user-friendly approach, sometimes with the assistance of international agencies. The substantial migratory movements ensuing the demise of Yugoslavia and latter conflicts in a region with a tradition of turbulence, together with changes in political administration are affecting spatial development and infrastructure requirements at both national and local levels and need a dual approach.

Read on: www.merr.sr.gov.yu;www.iaus.org.yu; www.uus.org.yu; www.gef.bg.ac.yu;
http://rcub.bg.ac.yu

FAST FACTS

- **Total Area:** 780,580 km²
- **Total Population:** 71,892,807
- **Population Growth:** 1.013%
- **Unemployment Rate:** 9.7%
- **GDP:** $667.7 billion
- **GDP per capita:** $9,400
- **GDP growth rate:** 5.1%

SETTLEMENTS STRUCTURE

- **Capital City:** Ankara
  3,456,100 pop
- **Second City:** Istanbul
  8,831,805 pop
  9,760,000 (metro. area)

- **Density:** 92 pop/km²
- **Urban Population:** 67%

Political and administrative organisation

Republic composed of 7 regions, 81 provinces and municipalities.

Administrative competence for planning

The State Planning Organisation represents the apex of a strongly centralised administrative system. The Ministry of Public Works and Housing, the Conservation Board of natural and cultural assets, and the housing development administration for mass housing are responsible for centralised planning and physical development. However some large scale regional developments are handled in parts by provinces. Cities and local authorities have been given competences for participation and some aspects of local ownership.

Main planning legislation

Bosphorus Law for environmental protection and cultural assets. Law 3194 of 1985 transferred responsibility for planning from central to local authorities, including for the Bosphorus to Istanbul. South eastern Anatolia project (GAP): 9 provinces responsible for mega-regional irrigation and hydroelectric strategy, including 22 dams and 19 hydro power plants. 2006 Law on Establishment, Coordination and Duties of Development Agencies. 2006 Regulation establishing city councils.

Planning and implementation instruments

The hierarchic and sectoral system consists of a national five year development plan; regional plans in some parts; land use plans; urban improvement plans, structure plans and implementation plans. They are very prescriptive and detailed. There are special plans for disaster areas, landfills on coasts, prevention of illegal settlements, urban improvement requested by municipalities, nature and conservation areas, and tourism. An integrated regional development plan exists for the Anatolia region with its own implementation powers.

Development control

Municipalities have only limited development control functions.

Planning system in practice

Squatter settlements (Gesekondu) have been a big problem in rapidly urbanising Turkey since the 1940s and still are. Despite legislation introduced in 1963 with later additions, including on land appropriation for post hoc retrofitting, it has not been applied in all areas and has led to unpredictable settlement development. The peculiar land ownership and tenure situation leads to large scale urban decay and frequent reconstruction, not just due to natural disasters. Turkey's regular exposure to natural disasters led to special risk assessment planning. There s a genuine need for decentralisation and more transparent local accountability, prerequisites for Turkey's accession to the European Union which would improve its economy.

Read on: www.bayindirlik.gov.tr; www.dpt.gov.tr; www.laud.bilkent.edu.tr; www.deu.edu.tr;
www.spo.org.tr; www.sbp.yildiz.edu.tr

LIST OF AUTHORS A-Z AND COUNTRIES

Adilova, Lyudmula	Uzbekistan	Eser, Thiemo	Luxembourg
Ajanovic, Asim	Bosnia	Ferrer, Mercedes	Venezuela
Ahmed, Adamu	Nigeria	Ferro Lozano, Ricardo	Colombia
Alaverdyan, Ruzan	Armenia	Fetahagic, Maida	Bosnia
Al-Hathloul, Saleh	Saudi Arabia	Figueroa, Jonas	Chile
Alleyne, Yolanda	Barbados	Fookes, Tom	New Zealand
Anderton, Christopher	Netherlands	Franchini, Teresa	Spain
Ankrah, Alexander	United Kingdom (Scotland)	Garay, Gonzalo	Paraguay
		Gargoum, Ammar	Lybia
Arana, Vladimir	Peru	Garon, Meir	Israel
Arroyo C., Víctor	Costa Rica	Gashi, Lumnije	Kosovo
Aubert, Bernard	France	Goedman, Jan C.	Netherlands
Bahreldin, Ibrahim Zakaria	Sudan	Golubovic Matic, Darinka	Serbia
Baires, Sonia	El Salvador	Goodman, Robin	Australia
Bardauskiene, Dalia	Lithuania	Gossop, Chris J.	United Kingdom
Bertran, M.	Chile	Green Castillo, Fernando	Mexico
Besio, Mariolina	Italy	Guet, Jean-Francois	France
Bishop, Andrew	Guyana	Hafiane, Abderrahim	Algeria
Brieva, A.	Chile	Halim, Deddy	Philipines
Brenes A., Daniel	Costa Rica	Ilmonen, Mervi	Finland
Burra, Marco	Tanzania	Inkoom, Daniel K. B.	Ghana
Butt, Abdul Manan	Pakistan	Islam, Muhammad Ariful	Bangladesh
Cace, Lolita	Latvia	Jamakovic, Said	Bosnia
Causarano, Mabel	Paraguay	Jokhadze, Natia	Georgia
Cavric, Branko I.	Botswana; Macedonia	Joergensen, Lars O.	Denmark
Crawford Jan	New Zealand	Junussova, Madina	Kazakhstan
Chabbi, Morched	Tunisia	Jurkovic, Sonja	Croatia
Chipungu, L.	Zimbabwe	Karunathilake, A. V. G. C.	Sri Lanka
Chowdhury, Tufayel Ahmed	Bangladesh	Khanlarov, Azer T.	Azerbaijan
da Costa Lobo, Manuel	Portugal	Kudryavtsev, Fedor	Russia
de Kock, Johan	Namibia	Kumata, Yoshinobu	Japan
Davies, John	United Kingdom (Wales)	Kyessi, Alphonce G.	Tanzania
Demires Ozkul, Basak	Turkey	Ledo, Carmen	Bolivia
Dhamo, Sotir	Albania	Lehzam, Abdellah	Morocco
Editors	Egypt; Greece	Leven, Rosie	United Kingdom (Scotland)
Elgendy, Hany	Germany	Lim, Seo-Hwan	Korea South
Ellul, Tony	Malta	Lin, John Chien-Yuan	Taiwan
Enotiades, Phaedon	Cyprus	Liu, Thai Ker	Singapore

Lusigi, Roswitha	Kenya	Sakano, T.	Japan
Magalhaes, Fernanda	Brazil	Sapatu, Fiona	Samoa
Maier, Karel	Czech Republic	Scholl, Bernd	Germany
March, Alan	Australia	Seraj, Toufiq M	Bangladesh
Mayo, Shaker Mehmood	Pakistan	Schloeth, Lucas	Switzerland
Merlo Robles, Lilian Regina	Guatemala	Schrenk, Manfred	Austria
Milosevic, Pedrag V.	Zimbabwe	Scornik, Carlos Osvaldo	Argentina
Moeller, Joergen	Denmark	Shaafi, Emhemed	Lybia
Molina, Nixon	Venezuela	Sihlongonyane, Mfaniseni	Lesotho; Swaziland
Murphy, Patricia	Maldivas	Snaggs, Keneth	Trinidad Tobago
Movahed, Khosrow	Iran	Soemoto, Sugiono	Indonesia
Nghi, Duong Quoc	Vietnam	Somova, Victoria	Kazakhstan
Niemczyk, Maria	Poland	Spiridonova, Julia	Bulgaria
Nollert, M.	Germany	Srinivas, Hari	Japan
Obregon Hartleben, Oliver	Guatemala	Stephen, Richard	USA
Odendaal, Nancy	South Africa	Suleiman, Moh'd Nageeb	Sudan
Oderson, Derrick	Barbados	Summers, Bob	Philipines
Olufemi, Olusola	Lesotho; Swaziland	Thors, Stefan	Iceland
Osman, Salah Mahmoud	Sudan	Trusins, Jekabs	Latvia
Osorio, María del Socorro	Honduras	ur Rahman, M. Atiq	Pakistan
Pacheco, Paola	Portugal	Van den Broeck, Jef	Belgium
Palmer, Karl G.	Sweden	van Ypersele, Joel	Belgium
Pallai, Katalin	Hungary	Viana, Isabel	Uruguay
Paskova, Miloslova	Slovakia	Vilas, Sara	Angola
Phiri, Daniel	Zambia	Wagener, Carmen	Luxembourg
Pichler-Milanovic, Natasa	Slovenia	Wang, Chi-Hsien	Taiwan
Pleho, Jasna	Bosnia	Wang, Liang Huew	Hong Kong
Preem, Martti	Estonia	Wilson, Barrie	Namibia
Rassam, Sahar	Iraq	Wiren, Erik	Sweden
Ribeiro, Edgard	India	Wohni, Arthur	Norway
Ricardo dos Santos, Cleon	Brazil	Wolfe, Jeanne	Canada
Ringli,Helmut;	Switzerland	Wyporek, Bogdan	Poland
Robinson, Peter	South Africa	Yunusa, Mohammed – Bello	Nigeria
Ross, Peter	China	Zeleza Manda, Mtafu A.	Malawi
Rubicki, Irene	Austria		
Russell, Paula	Ireland		
Ryden, Ewa	Sweden		
Ryser, Judith	Azerbaijan		

COLOPHON

Published by ISOCARP (International Society of City and Regional Planners)
P.O. Box 983, 2501 CZ, The Hague, The Netherlands
Email: isocarp@isocarp.org www.isocarp.org

First edition 1992, 2nd edition 1995,
third edition 1996, fourth edition 2001

Fifth new extended edition 2008

Editors: Judith Ryser & Teresa Franchini

Copyright © with the authors

All rights reserved

A catalogue record for this book is available from the British Library
ISBN: 978-90-75524-56-7
D.L.: M-49585-2008

Book & cover design and production by Paula Blanco Ballesteros
CD design and typeset by Dino Juloya
Website search by Maria Jose Roibon

Printed in Spain by Monterreina
Madrid, November 2008